The Partr

and

Allianc s

Audit

A Structured Assessment of Your Company's Existing and Proposed Joint Ventures and Partnerships

David Connell
The Technology Partnership Ltd.

Peter J. LaPlace
The University of Connecticut

Kenneth Wexler
New Business Search and Development, Inc.

FINANCIAL TIMES
Prentice Hall

An imprint of **PEARSON EDUCATION**

London · New York · San Francisco · Toronto · Sydney
Tokyo · Singapore · Hong Kong · Cape Town · Madrid · Paris · Milan · Munich · Amsterdam

PEARSON EDUCATION LIMITED
Head Office:
Edinburgh Gate
Harlow CM20 2JE
Tel: +44 (0)1279 623623
Fax: +44 (0)1279 431059

London Office:
128 Long Acre, London WC2E 9AN
Tel: +44 (0)207 447 2000
Fax: +44 (0)207 240 5771
Website: www.business-minds.com

First published in Great Britain 2000

Published in association with Cambridge Strategy Publications Ltd
39 Cambridge Place, Cambridge CB2 1NS.

ISBN 0 273 64715 6

British Library Cataloguing in Publication Data
A CIP catalogue record for this book can be obtained from the British Library

10 9 8 7 6 5 4 3 2 1

Typeset by Pantek Arts, Maidstone, Kent
Printed and bound in Great Britain

The Publishers' policy is to use paper manufactured from sustainable forests.

CONTENTS

INTRODUCTION

According to the traditional rules of management, competitors were enemies to be guarded against. Corporate leaders made conscious efforts to distance and protect themselves from other companies. If a capability was needed that wasn't available in house, managers tried to develop the function or purchase a company that excelled in that area.

The rules of the game have changed dramatically in the past ten years, however. Most executives now recognize the advantages of borrowing the capabilities of other companies, or collaborating with them on a less-than-fully-committed basis. Experience has shown that the development of trusting, cooperative relationships between companies can result in mutual benefit.

Strategic alliances, or collaborative ventures between businesses, have been popular since the mid 1980s. In the past, however, success rates, as measured by endurance of the partnerships and achievement of each company's goals for the alliance, have been relatively low. Those failures have occurred for a wide variety of reasons: in some cases, partners were not chosen strategically; in other cases, one partner's goals overtook the objectives of the other. In other instances, the partners may have relied on detailed legal agreements to ensure the success of the agreement, rather than developing strong personal relationships between appropriate people.

The experience of a high percentage of failures has created a substantial knowledge base about the factors that contribute to strategic alliance success. When alliances are planned carefully and managed well, they can produce great dividends, including the following benefits:

- A company may be able to introduce its products to markets that were previously inaccessible by teaming up with a company that already has a strong presence in that market. This is especially true in the case of cross-border or international alliances.

- Manufacturing or high-tech companies can collaborate on the development of new technologies. This allows both companies to bring a better product to market in much less time than under the old schema.

- Small companies can join forces to market their products or services in concert, thus providing the range of offerings of a large company with the flexibility and low cost of a small enterprise.

- Large companies can improve their cycle time and service to customers by developing collaborative relationships with their suppliers.

- Managers in both parent companies can increase their knowledge of effective techniques and practices. In Japanese companies, where the concept of strategic alliances has been practiced for a long time, an exchange of knowledge is often one of the primary motives for developing an alliance.

What a Strategic Alliance Audit Can Do

Given the historic high failure rate of strategic alliances (most estimates place it at over 60 percent), managers who are contemplating entering an alliance should look for ways to improve their chances for success. Companies who are already involved in alliances may be seeking ways of improving those partnerships. Although the audit guides presented here are generally framed in terms of evaluating a new alliance, the same variables should be assessed in order to measure the effectiveness of existing relationships. In many instances, revitalizing an ineffective partnership requires much the same process as coming to terms on a new alliance.

One of the keys to maintaining successful partnerships is to recognize that the relationship between the two companies (and the goals of that relationship) will be in a constant state of flux. Therefore, terms of the relationship must be re-negotiated when major changes occur in the elements affecting the partnership. For example, if the relative strength of one of the partners changes dramatically over time, roles and responsibilities in the partnership should be discussed and revised accordingly. On the other hand, the partnership need not be called a failure if frustrations and misunderstanding between the two partners arise during the course of the relationship. The audit guide presented here suggests probable trouble spots where partnerships may need to be fine tuned in order to function effectively.

This audit will now present two perspectives on strategic alliances. The first section discusses the evaluation of alliances for manufacturing firms, while the second focuses on service firms. Although some information is common to both sections, most managers should review both perspectives before initiating an audit, inasmuch as each contains valuable tips that are applicable to any alliance setting.

Part 3 looks at the audit process itself and provides a framework that addresses some of the logistical and process requirements of conducting an audit. Part 4 comprises a series of questions based on the steps in Parts 1 and 2. The questions are designed to help you plan and implement your audit in a straightforward and practical manner.

Part 1

THE STRATEGIC ALLIANCE AUDIT FOR MANUFACTURING FIRMS

The last ten years have seen a significant growth in the number of joint ventures and "strategic partnerships," particularly between manufacturing and technology-based companies. Types of alliances between companies include the following:

- Merging substantial components of a company's business, such as Honeywell-Bull or GPT.
- Strategic investing in business partners, such as General Motors' stake in Isuzu or Honda's investment in Rover.
- Creation of equity joint ventures to build new businesses, like British Telecom and Dupont's opto-electronics venture, known as BT&D.
- Investment in small companies involved in innovative new technologies, such as Monsanto's investments in companies like Collagen, Genex and Genentech.
- Using strategic trading relationships to build global distribution networks, such as Matsushita/JVC's supply of video recorders for resale under their own brands by RCA, Thorn-EMI and Thomson.

Strategic partnerships provide a powerful set of business tools of value to large and small companies alike. However, they do not always run smoothly. A study of 880 joint ventures and cooperative arrangements found that only 45 percent were found to be successful by *all* sponsors. Only three out of five ventures lasted for more than four years, and only 14 percent lasted more than ten years.[1]

At the same time, strategic partnerships are also increasing in diversity. Besides formal equity joint ventures, companies are getting together in a less permanent way to collaborate on Research and Development (R&D), teaming up to achieve major technological goals and splitting up later on to compete in specific applications. As technology becomes more complex, many companies are also finding it necessary to build relationships with suppliers that go far beyond traditional subcontracting. In the 1990s, manufacturing companies will be dominated by strategic partnering. Therefore, it is important to have a framework for evaluating and assessing their viability and to have means for improving them once they have been embarked on.

Two Key Questions

Although this audit provides extensive information on how to assess various factors which determine the success or failure of cooperative ventures, two questions are fundamental to this process:

- Are managers considering the use of partnerships in every situation where they can contribute to building competitive advantage?

- Are they planning, structuring and managing those partnerships effectively?

This section will provide tools for determining the answer to these questions for a given company.

What Are Strategic Alliances?

Strategic alliances are relationships between companies that may or may not involve equity or ownership arrangements. In many cases, a joint venture is created for the accomplishment of a particular task. However, the range of possibilities for developing alliances has grown tremendously in the last decade. While some partnerships are designed to endure, others are intended as temporary collaborations that accomplish specific goals.

The primary motivation for establishing most partnerships or alliances has been the need to respond to changes in the marketplace with ever increasing speed. Executives have learned that most companies lack the resources, technology, market access, or know-how to survive without the help of others. This is because each company and each management team has different strengths and weaknesses, different resources and different market knowledge. By establishing relationships with partners who can compensate for those weaknesses while benefiting from that company's strengths, managers can increase the efficiency with which their companies operate and respond to demands more quickly.

Alliances are an alternative to the traditional strategies of mergers or acquisitions. They allow companies to collaborate on relevant areas or projects, while pursuing different strategies or even competing directly in other parts of the business. Managing such a relationship presents some obvious challenges. Maintaining alliances requires a change in mindset, from the traditional view of competition to a new position of collaboration and cooperation. In many cases, both viewpoints must be held simultaneously. Alliances mean that control must be shared between two companies; most managers have been conditioned to seek complete control. However, the lesson to be learned from successful partnerships and alliances is that complete control often fails to produce superior management.

Establishing and maintaining an effective partnership with another company requires a great deal of energy and effort. The benefits of partnerships cannot be realized unless the relationship is carefully planned and thoughtfully managed. The steps that follow will provide insights into how this can be done.

STEPS IN CONDUCTING A STRATEGIC ALLIANCE AUDIT (MANUFACTURING)

Following the framework below will produce the information needed to evaluate a potential or existing strategic alliance in the manufacturing sector.

Step 1: Clarify the Objectives of the Alliance

Step 2: Evaluate the Plan for the Venture

Step 3: Specify Partner Criteria

Step 4: Screen and Investigate Partners

Step 5: Assess the Alliance Agreement

Step 6: Evaluate the Ability of the Alliance to Meet Changing Conditions

Each of these steps will be described in more detail.

Who Should Conduct the Audit?

In order to audit an alliance or evaluate an alliance prospect, a steering committee should be organized. The committee should be made up of an executive team member, a manager who is involved in the area of the business that will be most affected by a potential alliance, and another manager who has knowledge about or experience with the development of strategic alliances. The committee members should be chosen on the basis of their objectivity, judgment, and experience with the issues. Their ability to establish personal relationships with representatives from a prospective partner company should also be considered.

Step 1

CLARIFY THE OBJECTIVES OF THE ALLIANCE

Alliances are not strategic unless they contribute to the achievement of a company's overall objectives. There are a number of possible strategic objectives that can be achieved by developing alliances. Seven of the most common goals are described below.

Strategic Goal 1: Identify and Access New Technologies and Competencies

The accelerating pace of business innovation means that companies must be able to exploit important new technologies rapidly. One of the primary objectives of any industrial company must be to identify and monitor key technologies early in their development. This includes technologies which are likely to have a major impact on existing businesses, and technologies capable of creating new commercial opportunities. In other words, every business must monitor emerging product-market life cycle curves as they develop. Some of the developments will remain technological sideshows. Others could be major income earners in the future.

The competition to be first to exploit innovative technology is now so great that it is no longer possible to rely on in-house resources and the more traditional business development mechanisms of licensing and acquisition. To ensure long-term competitive advantage, companies must deploy a variety of mechanisms to locate and exploit external sources of research and development to augment their in-house commitments. The mechanisms available include:

- Collaboration with university departments and other research institutions.

- Pre-competitive collaborative R&D to spread research resources more wisely.

- Corporate venturing, or making systematic investments in emerging companies to gain a window on the technologies and market applications of the future; for example, many large pharmaceutical companies invested in small biotechnology R&D companies in the early 1980s before building up their own in-house teams.

- Joint ventures and other forms of strategic partnership which enable a company to acquire new competencies by "borrowing" them from a company with a leadership position.

Strategic Goal 2: Exploit New Market Opportunities Quickly and Effectively

Strategic alliances are critical to organization survival in today's environment. One of the key reasons for engaging in alliances is to learn about market and technological opportunities. Some of what will be learned affects a company's existing product range. Other learning affects its production methods. Well managed alliances, in combination with in-house R&D programs, will identify a steady stream of new commercial opportunities. Sooner or later, a company's leaders must decide whether those opportunities are attractive enough to get involved with commercially.

There are four main ways in which a company can enter a new market:

- In-house development.
- Licensing or sourcing product from an existing supplier, such as when Olivetti's first word processor was sourced from a small US hi-tech company in which it had invested.
- Acquiring an existing company.
- Joint venture with another company; many of Corning Glass's new businesses, like Siecor in fiber optic cables, have been created through equity joint ventures.

Speed is of the essence during the early phases of new product markets. Conventional large company organization structures are ill-suited to handling embryonic business opportunities, where the immediate outlook is rather uncertain and sales of only a few million dollars are likely over the first few years. Existing businesses and major contracts will always take precedence in decision making. It is difficult to allocate the best managers to business initiatives of this kind and hard to match the entrepreneurial environment of the thrusting start-up company. As a result, radical new business opportunities are often missed by large companies.

By contrast, independent entrepreneurial start-up companies can typically get new products to market faster and cheaper than the established multinational. Sourcing products from these sorts of companies under an OEM contract can offer a much quicker means of market entry.

Forming a new equity joint venture with a partner offering complementary skills can provide an attractive way of tackling opportunities which might otherwise fall by the wayside. It can also provide the autonomy required for new businesses operating in fast evolving and unfamiliar markets.

Joint ventures are particularly useful where a company has developed technology with commercial applications outside its core business and which it is not able to market effectively itself. British Telecom's 50:50 equity joint venture with Dupont to exploit opto-electronic component technology is a good example of this form of venture.

Strategic Goal 3: Build Market Position Rapidly

As product markets grow, the secret of competitive advantage moves away from the best technical and marketing solution towards market power. Remaining competitive in the long-term requires a scale of operations sufficient to support the high fixed costs of R&D, maintain strong advertising campaigns and retain the commitment of distributors. High sales volume also usually delivers low manufacturing costs through scale economies and learning curve effects.

One of the most important priorities for a company during the early growth period is to build market share before its competitors and provide the sales base from which to fight the rather different battles which will follow later. In many new markets, the ultimate winners are the companies that succeed in powering up this growth curve fastest. Basing this expansion entirely on 100 percent owned marketing resources is often too slow and expensive. Strategic marketing partnerships have an important role to play in expanding sales during this growth period, and particularly in establishing a strong position in export markets.

There are four different types of strategic partnerships which can help a manufacturer build market position rapidly:

- The supply of product on an OEM basis for rebadging and resale by other companies (*vertical supply alliances*); for example, Fujitsu supplies IBM compatible mainframes in the US through Amdahl and in Europe through Siemens; it also manufactures key components for ICL.

- The creation of *value added reseller networks*, where a range of different companies are involved in tailoring or augmenting the product for distribution to specialized users in various vertical markets.

- The establishment of *local joint ventures*, with or without a manufacturing capability, to access export markets; an example in Europe is J2T, a joint venture created by JVC, Thomson and Thorn EMI to manufacture video recorders.

- *Strategic investments* in local partners.

Besides helping a company maximize its own sales, these strategies can also help a company eliminate potential competitors by creating a network of distributors dependent on its technology. However, such strategies are also fraught with dangers. Many strategic partners are also potential competitors. The opportunity to resell or manufacture products could be the first step in developing their own. There is also a danger that by selling through others, a company can lose direct contact with its ultimate users and become insensitive to changing customer needs and opportunities.

In many markets, it is essential to consider entry and growth strategies together. This is especially true where new categories of product are being developed for sale to a market with a well defined customer base, or with well established international distribution channels. Examples include new generations of commercial airliners and most consumer electronics products. In these cases, it is possible by the judicious choice of development partners to ensure global market access from the start. Boeing's involvement of European and Japanese partners in recent projects and the Rolls Royce-led V2500 jet engine products are examples of this process.

In many areas of electronics, market success is also closely related with standards. There are often many competing standards during the early growth phase of new markets. But as the market matures, those standards with the greatest market share inevitably attract more attention from producers of associated equipment or software. This leads to a further dwindling in market support for manufacturers unlucky enough to have chosen the wrong standard at the start. In consumer electronics, telecommunications and information technology, some collaboration on standards prior to market entry is often essential to reducing risk. If partners are chosen carefully, this can create a de facto global standard, automatically easing entry to overseas markets while undermining the efforts of companies who have chosen to go it alone. Phillips' collaboration with Sony on compact disk standards is a good example.

Strategic Goal 4: Survive by Specializing

As markets move through the shakeout phase, suppliers become divided into the strong and the weak. The strong companies, like IBM in mainframe computers and Boeing in jet airliners, have an enormous advantage over the weaker group. The scale of their operations enables them to maintain much lower manufacturing costs. They can finance more R&D and be less preoccupied with its efficiency. They can sign up the best distributors and they can wield enormous political pressure.

Companies who are not in the first tier in terms of sales cannot hope to match the product development capabilities of their larger competitors through internal R&D. They may also be unable to match their production costs. Weaker companies must therefore adopt strategies which avoid direct competition with the market leaders.

There are five possible options:

- Specializing in a specific market sector or sub-product area.

- Switching to on-off contracts, in which scale economies are far less important.

- Buying in key components on an OEM basis.
- Becoming a subcontractor to the industry leaders.
- Becoming a distributor for the industry leaders.

Strategic alliances are important in each of the last three of these areas and can extend the ability of a company to compete as its markets mature. Aerospace, motor vehicles, computers, telecommunications and consumer electronics are all industries in which such alliances have been adopted. However, the erosion of either the R&D or marketing capabilities which these strategies often imply can have a serious long-term effect on innovation and competitiveness.

Strategic Goal 5: Re-Establish Critical Mass

As internationalization and competitive pressures increase, even large companies may find it simply impossible to compete with the industry leaders and remain totally independent. At this point, their only options are either disposal or some type of merger of operations with another company. Many companies are active in several business areas, each involved in markets of different maturity and each subject to different competitive pressures. Where a business unit is too small to be internationally competitive, undertaking a partial merger with a comparable division of another company can help strengthen market position and provide adequate R&D funding.

Partial mergers are particularly important in the European context, where the existence of national champions in each of the European economies has prevented the formation of corporations with the ability to compete in global markets. Examples include Alcatel, formed from CGE and ITT's telecommunications interests, and a series of partnerships between Britain's GEC and General Electric of the US. In aerospace, collaboration on specific projects performs a very similar function. In the case of Airbus Industrie, the collaboration has lasted so long as to produce what is essentially a new corporate entity.

Strategic Goal 6: Achieve Cost Leadership

As markets mature, competitors become more capable and a technology more established, price and cost increasingly dictate profitability. However, more is at stake in this process than simply the existing business. As a market grows, the cost of rejuvenating it through innovation increases. Gross margins need to be as high as possible, as quickly as possible, to finance this investment in the future. The shrinking of product market life cycles means that achieving cost leadership must be a priority from the start of any new business. Reducing costs must be an unrelenting task.

Strategic partnering can play an important role in this case as well. The objective is to pinpoint activities where sharing or subcontracting can reduce unit costs, either by setting up combined operations with competitors, or by disposing of assets which can be reinvested more effectively elsewhere in the business. Then outside companies should be used to fill the gap.

Carrying out these kinds of strategic cost reduction programs effectively requires a detailed understanding of the relationship between volume and cost in different parts of each of the company's businesses. For example, in the automobile industry, the greatest economies of scale are achieved in engine and gearbox manufacture. However, the key factors in consumer choice relate more closely to styling and overall value for money. Therefore, it is possible to collaborate in R&D in a way that does not inhibit a company from differentiating its products or adopting an independent marketing strategy. Programs to develop and manufacture these "hidden" components jointly therefore make a lot of sense for all but the largest manufacturers.

A further means of reducing unit costs is by sourcing products from low cost suppliers. To remain competitive as products mature, companies based in the advanced economies will increasingly need to work with NIC suppliers. In doing so, they face the danger of creating their own competitors. Equity partnerships provide an important means of internalizing this competition, either by joint venture or investment in the supplying company. For example, General Motors entered into a 50 percent joint venture with South Korea's Daewoo, which supplies the Pontiac Lemans for sale in the US.

At the same time, the cost benefits of subcontracting and collaboration must be weighed against the strategic risks of dependence on others, and the encouragement of competitors. Core skills and technologies must be closely guarded. Strategic investments and joint ventures can play a part in mitigating these risks, enabling a company to exert some degree of control over suppliers and distributors, as well as to participate in their success.

Strategic Goal 7: Withdraw from the Market in an Orderly Fashion

As the key to competitive advantage in each product market moves progressively towards scale and cost leadership, some companies inevitably find themselves fighting losing battles. Opportunities for refocusing the company as a specialist supplier or for acquiring shared economies of scale may be limited. Risks may also be great. The other units of the company may offer better opportunities; there may be insufficient cash available to fund all the investment required.

There are two traditional options in this situation: sell the business to another company, or gradually wind down operations. Partial mergers offer a third option, allowing phased disposal over perhaps three to five years to a competitor of similar size that is determined to remain in the business. In many circumstances, this can make disposal easier and more remunerative, as when brand names are shared with other parts of the company.

Alliances between manufacturing firms may be engaged in for any of these reasons. The importance of these goals in the audit process is to help the steering committee evaluate the objectives of an existing or prospective audit. This is the first step in assessing the effectiveness of a particular alliance.

Step 2

EVALUATE THE PLAN FOR THE ALLIANCE

Once the objectives of the alliance have been assessed, a more detailed plan should be evaluated in terms of its ability to support the objectives of the alliance. Managing strategic partnerships is very difficult. Although partnerships can make a powerful contribution to a company's future competitiveness, they must be approached in the right way. Each situation is different and each of the different forms of partnerships involve specific issues. However, there are a number of steps that can be taken to improve chances for success by improving the planning process.

While the plan for a strategic alliance may not be as detailed as the operating plan for a wholly-owned enterprise, certain planning procedures should be followed if the goals set out for the alliance are to be reached:

- Members of the steering committee should examine how the proposed or existing partnership is meant to help achieve the strategic goals set for their business. Before proceeding with or revising the alliance, the partnership should be compared with other easier alternatives in terms of costs, benefits, risks and speed of execution. Some possible alternatives include developing the resources in house that would be gained through the partnership, buying a company that would supply the same advantages, or pursuing a different strategy.

- The committee should review an outline of the activities to be undertaken within the partnership and the resources required. If such an outline does not exist, it can be easily generated by completing the worksheet in Figure 1. This *Key Resource Analysis* will help identify what contributions are sought from the partner and help evaluate the suitability of the current or prospective partners.

- The committee should study the broader relationships with the rest of the company's businesses and the long-term strategic impact. What resources have to be diverted from other areas in order to make the alliance work? How do customers and other stakeholders respond to the alliance? This study should include interviews with major customers and with industry experts. It should also solicit the input of key people within the company.

- Plan how the relationship is to be structured and managed to obtain optimum benefit. The structure of the relationship depends on what each partner brings to the alliance. A recent study by McKinsey and Company[2] found that alliances are most successful when ownership of the resulting enterprise is divided equally. This is because shared ownership implies shared responsibility. If ownership is not

FIGURE 1
KEY RESOURCE ANALYSIS

	BUSINESS OR NEW VENTURE REQUIREMENTS	KEY FACTORS FOR SUCCESS	INITIATING COMPANY CONTRIBUTION	IDEAL PARTNER CONTRIBUTION
Technology				
Product				
Market Access				
Marketing Capacity/Expertise				
Manufacturing Capacity/Expertise				
Customer Support				
Management				
Finance				
Other				

FIGURE 2
FINANCIAL RELATIONSHIPS FOR LOCAL MANUFACTURING & MARKETING JOINT VENTURE

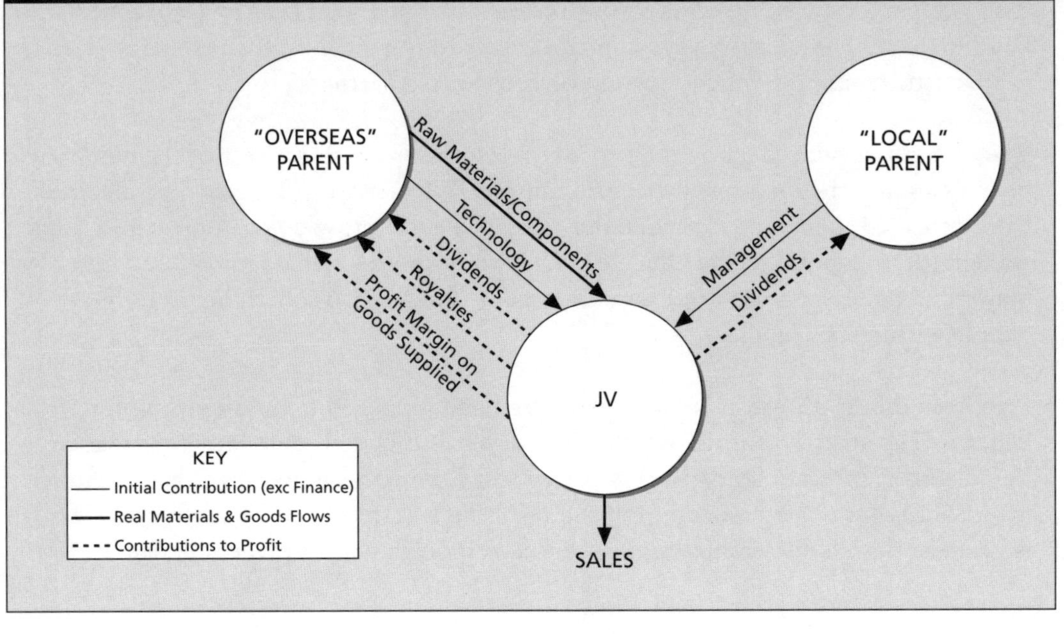

divided equally, then every effort should be made to develop a fair division of responsibility and ownership based on the contribution made by each of the partners.

- Model the financial arrangements and examine the impact of changes, as illustrated in Figure 2. This requires diagramming the contributions required of and rewards available to both partners in the alliance. This helps to clarify in the minds of the steering committee (and in the minds of partners) the expectations for the agreement.

This type of planning is critical to the success of any strategic alliance, regardless of its purpose.

Step 3

SPECIFY PARTNER CRITERIA

The exercise in Step 2, Figure 1, should have generated a partial list of the criteria needed in an ideal partner. The table completed as part of that exercise includes information about the specific strengths that are required for a particular partner. This section outlines some of the general considerations that should be taken into account when choosing an alliance partner. Alliance partners should be assessed according to these dimensions.

• *Company Size and Strength*

In many cases, larger companies engage in strategic alliances in order to tap new technologies or processes that have been developed in small, entrepreneurial firms. Large companies generally cannot develop new processes and products as rapidly as small companies can. In some cases, they may also be farther removed from the immediate market than are new start ups. On the other hand, small companies pursue alliances that will provide a source of income and possible access to large markets, as well as a source of knowledge that may help them improve their performance. For these reasons, alliances between large and small companies present a reasonable alternative.

However, a marriage between an extremely strong partner and a comparatively weak partner presents some obvious problems. Alliances in which one partner is consistently strong in the functions it brings to the venture while the other is not strong have a high failure rate. When one partner is weak, managing the alliance seems to be too great a distraction from improvements needed in other parts of the business. When unbalanced partnerships do succeed, it is usually because the strong partner brings the capability that is crucial to the venture; it pulls the weaker partner along for a while before acquiring it or finding another partner. *Therefore, the most effective partnerships seem to develop when the largest company is no more than three times the size of the smaller company.*

Alliances that are entered into with the purpose of strengthening the weaker partner have a high risk of failure. The dynamics of such an arrangement often lead to the domination of the alliance by the stronger partner. Partnerships tend to fail unless each partner has an equal stake in (and contribution to) the alliance.

• *Culture*

In order for partners to cooperate effectively, the companies must have compatible values and beliefs. Because the collaborative venture will be made up of people from both parent companies, they should approach work from similar perspectives if the alliance is to be successful. For example, serious conflicts may arise if one organization is highly bureaucratic while the other one shuns policies and procedures. If the culture of one parent is highly competitive and the other stresses cooperation, managers from the two companies may find it difficult to work together.

Some cultural values lend themselves better to alliances than others. Two of the values that are conducive to good alliances are described below.

— *Flexibility.* The mark of a good alliance is one that can change as conditions evolve. This is only possible when both partners are willing and able to make concessions and compromises as their ability to contribute to the alliance changes. They must also be willing to accept the modifications required when the other company's ability to contribute changes.

— *Ability to transfer skills.* Companies involved in a partnership must be able to transfer skills, and implement the skills derived from the knowledge base offered by the other company. A company that can receive but not transfer skills may not be able to integrate new staff from the partner company into their organization. A company that can transfer but not receive skills usually has a top-down management style and may not adapt well to changes required by the other partner. An ideal alliance partner can both receive and transfer skills.

• *Complementarity of Businesses*

Alliances tend to be ineffective when they center on the core business of either of the partners. Likewise, they are more useful for breaking into new markets, rather than operating in markets where both companies already have a strong presence with competing products. Some of the best partnerships result when one company contributes a unique technology and the other partner provides access to a market previously untapped by the technology-bearing company. In other successful cases, the companies have collaborated on the development of new technology that is related to the core businesses of both partners, but does not directly compete with either business.

• *Management Compatibility*

In the past, too many managers have depended on the details of the partnership contract to work out problems that arise during the life of the alliance. Research shows that a more effective approach is for the managers from each parent company who will have responsibility for the alliance to develop strong personal relationships. The initiation of such relationships should take place during the process of investigating prospective partners. Executives should not underestimate the importance of personal chemistry in choosing alliance partners. These personal relationships will be vital to the resolution of problems that develop in the alliance at later stages.

Step 4

SCREEN AND INVESTIGATE PARTNERS

Information Sources on Alliance Partners

The selection of an appropriate alliance partner may come about spontaneously through informal ties between technology or management staff. In cases where the choice of a partner is not obvious, however, there are a few systematic approaches that will ensure that executives have explored a wide range of possibilities, thus increasing the probability of finding a match that approaches the ideal. Those approaches include the following:

- Consult industry experts. Analysts who are familiar with the industry may suggest companies who match the criteria outlined for the partnership. They may also be able to provide input on the compatibility of potential partners once the list of prospects has been narrowed.

- Review trade publications. This may include an electronic data base search for companies within appropriate industries. The search can be narrowed by using key terms drawn from the profile developed for the ideal partner.

- Consult trusted customers or suppliers. Those who work closely with the company may be able to suggest partners who would provide the qualities needed for an effective alliance.

Once a list of prospective partners has been made, they should be assessed against the criteria developed for the partnership. Company literature should be solicited from each of the candidates as a preliminary tool for evaluating their compatibility. Industry experts, both inside and outside the company, should also be approached for their input into the decision.

The list of candidates should be narrowed to between three to five candidates, who should be contacted by the initiating company. Executive-level representatives of the candidate companies should be contacted to assess interest and ability to provide what is required by the alliance.

Evaluating the Suitability of Each Candidate

For those companies who appear on the short list of alliance partner candidates, the initiating company should engage in a considerable amount of due diligence research. This research may include the following steps:

- Interview the company's major customers. How well do they meet customer needs? Do they respond quickly and effectively to the demands of the market?

- Obtain a credit report for each of the final candidates.

- Evaluate the distribution of sales for each of the candidates. Is the company overly dependent on one customer? Are their sales concentrated in markets to which the initiating company wants to gain access?

- What is the potential partner's reputation in the industry? Are they known for following through on their agreements, or do they pose risks that the initiating company should avoid? What is their reputation in terms of developing new technology?

- Do executives at the prospective partner seem interested in and committed to making an alliance work? Do their goals for the alliance match up with the objectives of the initiating company?

The selection or evaluation process will evolve as new information is acquired. Prospective partners may be deleted from the list or added to it as the process continues. Alliances should be approached in much the same way that a marriage is approached. The relationship should be looked at from a long-term perspective, with an emphasis on the partners' ability to respond to changing conditions.

Step 5

ASSESS THE ALLIANCE AGREEMENT

When candidates compare favorably with the criteria set out for the audit, then it is time for the steering committee to evaluate the process and details of developing the detailed alliance agreement. An effective process will include the following elements:

Letter of Intent

The letter of intent should outline the general goals and objectives of each of the parent companies for the alliance. It should also describe the form of the alliance and the contribution of each parent in general terms. It should be agreed upon by executives from both companies.

Business Plan for the New Venture

The business plan should be developed by working teams from each of the parent companies. The working teams should be composed of people who will manage the new venture once it begins operation. The plan should include information that would be provided in the plan for any new venture, including market analysis, a marketing plan, financial projections, descriptions of the management team, etc. Research sources include data gathered from both parent companies, from customers and industry experts, and from secondary sources, such as trade publications or on-line data bases.

Among the last sections of the business plan to be developed should be a detailed description of what the contributions of each of the partners will be. As the business plan evolves, it should be reviewed by executives from each of the parent companies at each major iteration. It may be useful to have the plan presented to the respective executives by a neutral third party as insurance that feedback given on the plan is honest. This will increase the chances that the agreement fully satisfies the needs and expectations of both partners.

Final Agreement

If the final agreement grows out of a well-researched business plan, then the success of the venture is more likely. The agreement should be based on the needs of the venture rather than on the political maneuvering of the respective partners. This contributes to the establishment of a healthy relationship between companies and ensures that the resources and skills needed to build a successful alliance are available.

In the most effective alliances, the formal agreement plays an insignificant role. Although it provides a starting point for the alliance, the alliance agreement is a notoriously ineffective tool for resolving problems that arise in the partnership as it grows and evolves. In most alliances that are effective over the long run, changes are negotiated on the basis of personal relationships between representatives from each company rather than on the technicalities of the alliance agreement.

Step 6

Evaluate the Ability of the Alliance to Meet Changing Conditions

Although each situation differs, managing any strategic partnership presents difficulties. If alliances have been designed according to the steps in this audit, however, they will have a good chance of succeeding. The hallmark of a successful alliance is one that changes over time. Assessing a company's performance in terms of the following seven rules enable the steering committee to evaluate the alliance's ability to respond as conditions evolve.

1. Balance Trust with Self-Interest.

Establishing a relationship of mutual trust between partners is one of the keys to any successful partnership. If planning ensures that the right machinery has been constructed to make a partnership successful, it is mutual trust that greases the wheels. Genuine trust is based on the following factors:

- A mutual understanding of the partner's business; knowing what the other partner is capable of delivering.

- An mutual appreciation of the partner's objectives.

- Good personal relationships.

The partner's short-term objectives need to be understood because it is important that they be achieved. All partners must feel that they stand to benefit if the strategic partnership is to get off the ground in the first place. Pushing for the best "deal" without regard to the other partner's interests merely sours the relationship before it has had a chance to bear fruit.

At the same time, partners should try to look at how the partnership fits into the other company's long-term strategy. For example, what are the other company's aspirations with regard to the partner's business or markets?

Evaluating a company's ability to work effectively with another management team is an important component in any successful strategic partnership. The negotiating period is critical to evaluating these personal relationships. Getting to know the partner's key personnel socially early on helps ensure that any potential difficulties that may arise can be aired frankly and solved in an atmosphere of mutual self-interest, rather than confrontation.

2. Anticipate Strategic Conflicts

Companies entering strategic partnerships must try to identify the potential for conflicts and second-guess any hidden agendas that a partner might have. Partners must look carefully at the other parent's overall strategy and at any other partnerships in which the other business may be involved. Some companies might try to use a combination of alliances as a springboard to build up in-house capabilities and mount a competitive attack on their partner's business.

Understanding the webs of alliances that most multinational companies are spinning today is a complex task. It is often impossible to find partners with whom a potential conflict of some kind does not exist. Understanding where potential conflicts exist can help establish areas where action must be taken to reduce competitive risks.

Where a formal joint venture is formed, the scope of business must be very clearly defined to make sure that the potential for competition with the parent companies can be managed effectively.

One of the most important risks is unplanned seepage of technology. Any strategic partnership is somewhat like a semi-permeable membrane through which technology and expertise can flow unintentionally from the stronger partner to the weaker. An audit should look for any apparent leaks in the system. One way to reduce technological seepage is to divide the project into carefully defined components so as to make the collaboration as "vertical" as possible. The audit should consider the partner's access to resources and personnel. The limits of the relationship should be defined to ensure that staff know what information can be shared and what information cannot.

3. Establish Clear Strategic Leadership

Clear leadership is essential in any business or project, and one of the most important aspects of structuring a strategic partnership is choosing the right leader. Ineffective leadership makes coordination difficult and expensive; it slows down development, and it can make it virtually impossible for important decisions to take effect. One sign of strategic leadership is the creation of an independent entity headed up by a strong, politically adept chief executive or project director. Airbus Industrie, BT&D, MCC and ICOT are examples of this approach.

A second sign of clear strategic leadership is when one of the partners takes on the role of project management. This is the easiest solution in major development projects requiring the integration of complex inputs from many partners. It also helps speed the process of integration in partial mergers.

4. Learn Flexible Management

Companies involved in strategic partnerships should demonstrate an ability to manage without the kind of control to which they are accustomed. The degree of influence a company has depends very much on the type of partnership and on the power balance that exists between partners. A company's influence can also change over time. For example, a minority investor in a company that is doing well has little or no influence over its management. On the other hand, a company that is performing poorly while looking for sales or an injection of capital must listen carefully to its stakeholders.

The degree of involvement venture capitalists have in the companies they invest in fluctuates according to the phase and condition of the project: they offer advice and the injection of key business skills during periods of development; they keep an arm's length relationships when things are going well; and they have to be able to demand changes in management if things are going badly.

Companies involved in strategic partnerships should show the same kind of flexibility. Regular communication should take place on a number of different levels to make this possible. Managers must be both diplomatic and astute. Companies must ensure that all members of their team understand the importance of working with the other partner constructively. At the same time, the limits of cooperation must also be clear; sensitive information must be identified and isolated. Self-interest should always come first. Companies must be prepared to demand tighter control or change partners if the partnership is not delivering the benefits sought.

5. Accommodate Cultural Differences

The potential for cultural conflict abounds in strategic partnerships. Conflict can arise in a number of different ways. There are differences between large and small company management styles; there are differences between national business cultures; and there are differences between the management styles of established corporations.

Differences between the large and small company styles of management are one of the major causes of difficulty in corporate venturing. Large companies tend to have complex structures with multiple tiers of management, and they tend to have established procedures for making investment decisions. There are usually many different groups with an interest in any given project, slowing down decision making. In small companies, where regular day-to-day contact between employees makes informal communications the norm for exchanging information, decisions can be made quickly by just one or two people.

There are enormous and well documented differences between western and Japanese business cultures. However, there are also many differences among the business cultures of western nations. For example, US companies tend to enter legal discussions at an earlier point in negotiations than do European companies, and their executives are often more direct than a European manager would be.

Evaluating a partner's business culture is an important part of the audit process. Evaluating the ability of both companies to resolve cultural differences is also important. Although companies should seek partners with appropriate cultural characteristics, bridging cultural gaps requires understanding and forbearance. It is important that all members of the partnership team know what is involved. They should know how their partner makes decisions and where the limits of authority lie. They must also try to understand their partner's procedures for planning and measuring performance, and its rules for social and business behavior.

6. Orchestrate Technology Transfer

The creation or transfer of new technology is an important objective of many strategic partnerships. Such partnerships are often initiated by the technical staff within the parent organizations. Collaborative R&D programs are usually the children of their sponsors' R&D department. Communications within corporate venturing relationships are generally first formed at a technical level in order to enable investors' R&D people to evaluate the venture's technology. Commercial exploitation of the results of these efforts requires communication in the opposite direction — back to the parent companies — and to technical functions.

In many partnerships, channels of communication at the commercial level are created too late. And communications problems are exacerbated by the turnover of managers, with key decision makers on both sides being replaced on average every three to five years.

A technology transfer plan should be available to ensure that the technology developed is brought back into the sponsoring company, and that its commercial potential is well promoted internally. Each partner should have a strong "receptor" team with the technical skills to understand and use the technology. As the technical and marketing uncertainties are reduced and the technology or product comes closer to commercial exploitation, contact with the receptor team must increase.

7. Learn from the Partner's Strengths

Every company has a different way of doing things. All companies can learn from others. Strategic partnerships offer the opportunity to observe how another company operates — the way R&D programs are managed, how the business development program is organized, how management information systems operate, how overseas subsidiaries are managed and even how remuneration packages are determined. For example, many companies in the UK automotive components industry are now setting up partnerships with Japanese suppliers whereby they can learn Japanese manufacturing and product development methods.

Partners in an alliance should be evaluated in terms of their ability and willingness to learn. Institutionalized learning does not happen automatically. The right mechanisms must be in place to make it happen. At least some of the individuals involved in strategic partnerships must be chosen for their receptivity to new ideas, as well as for their ability to disseminate what they have learned throughout the organization. Internal seminars must be set up to spread this knowledge; special programs must be created to evaluate the relevance of this knowledge to the company's particular circumstances; and career patterns must be planned to ensure that ideas are rapidly passed on and implemented in key locations.

Direct experience teaches most effectively. The more effective mechanisms there are for people to be involved in the learning experience that strategic partnerships provide, the sooner change will be made back home.

SUMMARY

The pace of business innovation — not just technological innovation — is accelerating. Companies must focus on better ways of staying ahead — on being first to exploit new technologies and markets; on building global distribution networks before their competitors; and continually finding new ways of reducing operating costs.

An inevitable result of this acceleration is that there will be a faster turnover in companies' business portfolios. Today's technological lead soon begets tomorrow's price war. Today's cash cow soon turns into tomorrow's dog. No company can expect to have all the resources — technical, financial and managerial — to respond to this fast changing environment quickly enough. Acquisition is too inflexible and too unwieldy a tool to achieve every business development objective.

Strategic partnering offers an increasingly important response to this more complex, more urgent and less forgiving competitive environment. However, there are many pitfalls for the inexperienced. It is often more difficult than managers first imagine to deliver real commercial or strategic benefits from situations in which control is split between two or more partners. Objectives and priorities can change over time. Sometimes the easiest partnerships to negotiate are those with the most significant hidden agendas, where one partner is using the alliance to acquire new competencies for its core business. Taking advantage of the offers, and coming out on top, is one of the most important challenges CEOs will face in the 1990s. Auditing alliances and alliance prospects in terms of the elements presented in this guide is one way of enhancing the chances of success.

Part 2

THE STRATEGIC ALLIANCE AUDIT FOR SERVICE FIRMS

Keiretsu in Japan, joint ventures in the United States and Europe, cooperative buying arrangements, R&D consortia and numerous other forms of alliances are quite common in today's business environment. These alliances have been used for many years among manufacturing companies and have gained popularity among service firms in the past decade. Despite the growth in the number of almost all forms of alliances, many fail to achieve their objectives. When this happens, managers must disassociate the parent firms, patch up their wounds, and try to determine what went wrong.

The types of alliances most commonly used in service firms are described below. While each of these forms may differ in its purpose and composition, there are a few characteristics that tend to distinguish successful alliances from those that fail. This audit presents a systematic procedure for assessing strengths and weaknesses among a service company's existing and prospective alliances. While alliances are difficult to develop and consume a great deal of management time, most major service companies now see them as a critical component for achieving corporate growth objectives.

Service Companies as the Focus

The service sector encompasses a wide variety of industries. Service revenues have consistently increased as a percentage of Gross Domestic Product in many of the countries in the industrial world triad (North America, Europe and the Far East). There is also a major expansion of service provisions by companies whose primary offering is products. Joseph Fuller of Monitor Company, a Boston-based consulting firm, has noted that most companies in today's environment do not create value for customers and sustainable advantage for the enterprise by offering varieties of products, but by attaching services to those products.[3] As governments continue to expand, there has also been a dramatic increase in the number and size of firms that supply services to government agencies and government programs. Major types of service offerings include the following:

The rest of this assessment will be devoted to a discussion of how managers can evaluate their current and prospective alliances. The information gathered from the audit should provide useful insights into making the alliances more effective.

STEPS IN CONDUCTING A STRATEGIC ALLIANCE AUDIT (SERVICES)

Most large firms are currently engaged in strategic alliances. A recent Anspach Grossman Portugal study indicated that companies with more than $1 billion in sales had a median of five alliances or joint ventures. The steps that are described below can be used to evaluate the effectiveness of those alliances, and provide direction about how to improve them. They can also be used to design better new alliances.

Step 1: Determine the Appropriate Type of Alliance

Step 2: Determine Customer Requirements and Establish Criteria

Step 3: Evaluate Suitability of Current or Potential Partners

Step 4: Initiate Relationship With Selected Candidates

Step 5: Develop Relationship With Prospective Candidates

Step 6: Evaluate the Formal Agreement

Step 7: Evaluate the Post-Agreement Relationship

Each of these steps will be described in greater detail.

Who Should Conduct the Audit?

The audit should be initiated and supported by a member of the executive team. This will signal the importance of the evaluation to others in the organization. The bulk of the audit work is usually carried out by a team of several people from within the company who understand the details of developing alliances, and yet who have no vested interest in the success or failure of the particular alliance under consideration. Objectivity among the audit team members ensures that both the flaws and the strong points of an alliance will be reported clearly and fairly. The final product resulting from the audit should be a brief report (usually about ten pages) summarizing the audit findings and presenting recommendations for improving or establishing the alliance.

Step 1

DETERMINE THE APPROPRIATE TYPE OF ALLIANCE

Alliances are informal and/or formal relationships (more than a buyer/seller relationship and less than a total ownership position) between two or more firms, established for *mutual advantage*. An alliance will perform according to its purpose and structure. Therefore, the first step in the alliance audit process should be to clarify the purpose and nature of the relationship.

Types of Alliances

Alliances offer managers less control than they would have with activities owned 100 percent by the company. At the same time, they offer more flexibility and shared responsibility for the achievement of a particular objective. They often involve a partial equity position.

Alliances for services firms are distinct in certain ways from the alliances typically entered into by manufacturing and product-oriented companies. The major distinction is that service companies generally focus on the marketing and distribution benefits of alliances, while manufacturing firms usually focus on the technology transfer benefits of alliances.

There are four major types of alliances for services companies:

- Alliances for *new-to-the-world services development*, or working together to develop new service offerings not currently offered by anyone.

- Alliances for services *offering expansion* , or working together to improve or expand the types of services available from the alliance partners to their existing customers.

- Alliances for *customer base expansion,* or working together to expand service provision to new customers, new markets, or new countries/regions.

- Alliances for coordination of *sequential service offerings*, which happens when small, specialized firms team up to offer expanded services to a single client.

Descriptions and examples of each of these types of alliances are provided below.

New-to-the-World Service Alliances

While development of new services through an alliance offers less control than internal development, it may reduce each partner's need to invest in market research, concept development, service offering development, and development of the capabilities to perform, market and sell a new service. Examples of this type of alliance include the following:

- In August of 1993, Bell Atlantic Corp. announced an alliance with a tiny company called CellularVision of New York Inc. The alliance will use an innovative microwave technology developed by CellularVision to permit Bell Atlantic to deliver multimedia services using a flat, four-square-inch antenna that is mounted on a window and that costs about half as much to install as cable television.

- The Motorola-led Iridium alliance for provision of worldwide cellular service is another massive set of alliances designed to increase the ability of its members to provide new technology.

- Digital Media recently compiled a six-page list of this type of alliance growing up around the development of interactive television.

Service Offering Expansion Alliances

This type of alliance may permit a firm to offer new services supplied by an alliance partner, either sold through their own sales efforts, or sold in tandem with their partner's sales efforts. This is sometimes known as "Cross-Selling", and can work in many different forms.

- General Electric Capital Mortgage Corporation (Raleigh, North Carolina) and North American Mortgage Corporation (Santa Rosa, California) are two mortgage banking firms that formed this type of alliance in 1988. North American can supply both mortgage banking and loan servicing to its customers due to its alliance with General Electric. North American started out as a customer of GE's mortgage insurance business; this business has expanded 1000 percent since 1988. In addition, GE now conducts a substantial amount of loan servicing for North American (technically known as "flow servicing"). In return, GE also supplies North American with working capital. GE also recently began purchasing jumbo loans from North American.

  GE's approach was to transform a customer into a strategic partner by paying greater attention to its specialized needs. In a related acquisition, Travelers Mortgage Services, Inc. gave GE the servicing technology it needed to expand the North American alliance.

- Universal Systems Inc. (Fairfax, Virginia, US), provides another example of this type of alliance. Universal is a value-added computer systems reseller and systems integrator that works at any one time with 20 or 30 vendors. Beyond the normal buy-sell provisions of these arrangements, Universal helps the vendors understand their customers' needs. The vendors offer technical support, maintenance services and ready accessibility.

- To entice its customers to shop more during lunch and dinner hours, The Home Depot (a large do-it-yourself and contractor building supply retailer in the US) is discussing the possibility of installing mini-McDonald's restaurants in some of its stores. Customers, both homeowners and contractors, would be able to grab a quick bite to eat while shopping at the building materials specialist.

- Another example of this type of alliance is the development of PMHOs (physician-multi-hospital organizations) in Radnor, Pennsylvania (US). These are economic entities jointly owned by a hospital system and one or more physicians' associations. One PMHO provides a formal structure for coordinating decision making with respect to managed care contracting and development of non-hospital community services. The alliance permits the patient (customer) to benefit from a wider range of services and the economies of scale inherent in the coordinated packaging and pricing of physician-hospital services.

- In the television network industry, New Britain, Connecticut-based WVIT-TV (NBC) recently agreed to an alliance with Waterbury, Connecticut-based WTXX-TV (Fox). The NBC affiliate will supply the Fox affiliate with a 10.00 p.m. local news show.

Customer Base Expansion Alliances

This form of alliance may permit partners to surmount barriers to entry, coordinate distribution systems, or develop a joint sales force. In international markets, it may help secure a foothold where partners may be legally required. Examples of this type of alliance are as follows:

- British Airways (BA) made an investment in USAIR in early 1993. They made a \$300 million investment, purchasing 21.8% of USAIR Group's voting equity, and placing three members on its 16-member board of directors. This alliance benefits both BA and USAIR in continuing their goals of global expansion. It also provides a financial boost to USAIR. An interesting customer benefit of the alliance is something the airline industry calls "code sharing". In many cases, some of the true benefits of alliances are somewhat technical and industry-specific in nature. These benefits may not be obvious to the casual outside observer. In this case, a governmental agreement between the United States and the United Kingdom authorized British and U.S. reservation systems to jointly show the USAIR and BA codes in their computers for USAIR flights that connect in U.S. cities to BA overseas flights. This permits agents to book a complex itinerary with simplified reservation and fare quote procedures, coordinated schedules to minimize connection times, one-point check-in for transatlantic passengers, and easier coordination of frequent flyer programs.

- BT PLC, a UK telecommunications service firm, acquired a partial interest in MCI Communications in June of 1993. This allowed for the international expansion of BT PLC's customer base.

- In the Pittsfield, Massachusetts (US) area, numerous custom plastic molding service providers formed an alliance to conduct joint marketing efforts. These small firms were able to secure larger orders and divide the work among themselves.

Sequential Service Offerings Alliances

These alliances permit companies to work together to coordinate a sequence of services. This facilitates the delivery of a complete package to the customer. This type of alliance provides for coordination of services where there is a required sequence in which the services must be performed. For example, a series of small promotional firms may collectively serve as a full-service advertising agency. One firm may provide creative services, a second media purchases, a third could supervise printing and layout, and a fourth might monitor the results of the advertisements. Other examples are described below:

- A three-person commercial art company has formed an alliance with a commercial photographer and a graphics print shop to capture the contract for producing all of the brochures for one of the largest art museums in the world. Members of this alliance shoot pictures of exhibit material, have pictures approved by the museum staff, design coordinated brochures, letterheads, envelopes and other printed material, and produce a superior finished product which meets the museum's standards of excellence.

- A small machine shop that features ultra-high precision machining (a service performed on the customer's product) has entered an alliance with an advanced coatings service company. The coating service company applies a precision thermal coating to parts the other partner has machined for a major original equipment manufacturer (OEM). Due to rigid just-in-time requirements, these two partners must carefully coordinate their schedules to ensure that completed parts will arrive as needed.

- A builder or remodeler may form an alliance with a bank to provide construction loans and/or second mortgages for residential customers using the builder's services.

The four major types of services alliances are noted in Figure 3.

FIGURE 3
ALLIANCES FOR SERVICE COMPANIES

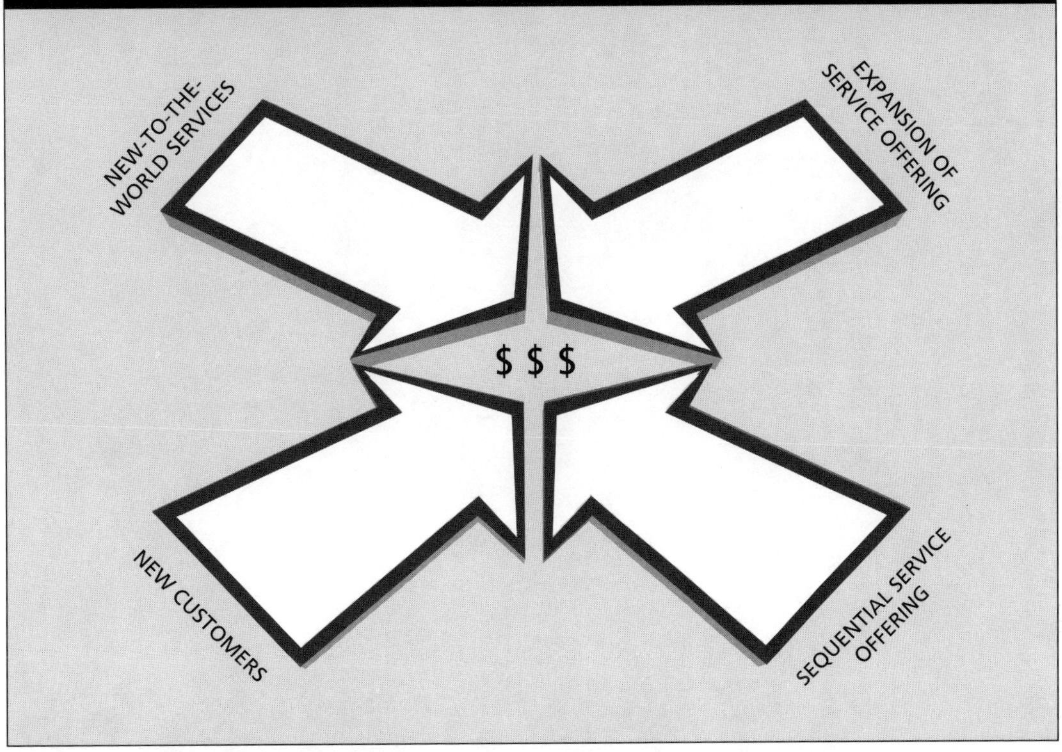

Benjamin Gomes-Casseras, Harvard professor, summarizes the purpose of service alliances succinctly: "*The whole point is to get selective access to capabilities you need that are embedded in another company.*"[4]

Another way to categorize alliances is by their planned lifetime of survival and where the results of the alliance will reside. Professor Peter Lorange and his colleagues at the Norwegian School of Management propose that it is possible to define a continuum of the types of alliances[5] based on this notion.

At the less intense end of the continuum are *ad hoc* and *consortium* alliances, in which each alliance partner contributes resources on a temporary basis, and all of the output is given back to the parents. At the more intense end of the continuum are *project-based ventures* and *full-blown joint ventures*, in which the main outputs of the alliance are retained in the venture. Almost all alliances require an extensive amount of additional management time and cannot be controlled completely by any of the partners. They generally require more management time than an internal venture. This investment is justified by the benefits that derive from a good alliance.

Step 2

DETERMINE CUSTOMER REQUIREMENTS AND ESTABLISH AUDIT CRITERIA

Successful service alliances provide the end customer with better value (new services, lower cost, higher quality, reduced time, etc.) *Therefore, an audit of alliance effectiveness must carefully identify, and if possible quantify, the factors that are of value to the end customer.* These requirements should direct the establishment of criteria for evaluating the alliance.

Determining customer requirements may involve surveys (in the case of broad markets with many customer) or discussions with specific customers (in the case of narrow markets with few customers). These inquiries should focus on broad customer needs, such as what services the customer would like to buy that are not currently offered by either the parent companies or the alliance.

Auditors should also tap other important sources of information, such as prospective customer groups and industry experts. Good sources of general information about the market niche that the alliance competes in include trade journals, trade show participation, and commercial market data (purchased either from an on-line research service or from market analysts). This will help auditors to determine customer needs and preferences, as well as to identify successful service providers operating in the market.

Another important part of assessing customer needs is to identify specific requirements that may bar customers from buying the output of an existing or proposed alliance. Individual customers may place restrictions on the type of company that can be part of an alliance. For example, some customers may have strict policies barring the participation of foreign-owned companies. Others may exclude unionized companies. In other instances, customers may require that alliance partners have government clearance.

Establishing Alliance Criteria

Once research about general market demands has been completed, the audit team should outline the basic requirements for the alliance. These requirements should be outlined both in terms of customer needs and in terms of the kind of alliance partner that would make the greatest contribution to the alliance. These criteria can most easily be established by first clarifying the objectives and purposes of the alliance.

The initial criteria and objectives for the alliance can guide the decision process not only in establishing the partnership, but also in the management and revision of the alliance. These criteria may change as the partnership evolves. At this phase of the audit, criteria should be developed that consider some or all of the following elements:

- what types of markets should be served
- types of services to provide
- whether the service should be fully developed from the outset or whether they should be developed as part of the alliance
- the geographic area(s) of interest and exclusion
- sales goals
- financial criteria (returns) and the ability of the partners to invest
- date of first commercial sale
- leveragable strengths of the initiating firm
- leveragable strengths needed in the alliance partner(s)

FIGURE 4
STRATEGIC ALLIANCE CRITERIA RANKING

CRITERION	MUST HAVE	DESIRABLE	BONUS
Established presence in Korean markets			
Reputation for technology excellence			
Good market research know-how			
Interest in developing similar technologies			
Annual sales between US$15 million and US$50 million			
Excellent reputation in customer support			
Ability to finance half of the alliance			
Korean-speaking management			

- size of the alliance partner (in general, alliances have greater chances of succeeding when partners are of roughly equal size)

The table in Figure 4 can be used to rank the criteria according to the priority they hold in the alliance. It includes sample criteria that might be set by an audit team for a small engineering firm hoping to increase its sales to Korea and develop critical new technologies.

Once the criteria for partner selection have been established, they can be used to audit the quality of the existing relationship, or to search for a new partner for a prospective alliance. This process will be described in the following pages.

Step 3

EVALUATE SUITABILITY OF CURRENT OR POTENTIAL PARTNERS

In the case of existing alliances, partners with whom the initiating company is involved should be evaluated in terms of their appropriateness for the alliance being pursued. As described earlier in this chapter, the use of an inappropriate partner may be one factor in the failure of an alliance. In other cases, it may be necessary to re-negotiate the terms of the agreement and work to rebuild trust that has been destroyed because of ineffective functioning of the alliance. This audit step can help to identify points of ineffectiveness or areas where re-negotiation may be necessary. This process should be repeated regularly throughout the life of an alliance, as conditions affecting the relationship between companies change constantly.

In the case of new alliances, every effort should be made to select partners that most closely approach the ideal. The specific criteria outlined in Step 2 should be taken into consideration, along with the following general factors:

- *Ability to Contribute Equally to the Alliance*

A marriage between an extremely strong partner and a comparatively weak partner presents some obvious problems. Likewise, alliances should be avoided where one partner has a much greater commitment to the relationship in comparison to the other partner or partners. Alliances in which one partner is consistently strong in the functions it brings to the venture while the other is not strong have a high failure rate. When one partner is weak, managing the alliance seems to be too great a distraction from improvements needed in other parts of the business. When unbalanced partnerships do succeed, it is usually because the strong partner brings the capability that is crucial to the venture; it pulls the weaker partner along for a while before acquiring it or finding another partner. Therefore, *the most effective partnerships seem to develop when the largest company is no more than three times the size of the smaller company*, when all partners are equally committed to the alliance, and when the strengths and weaknesses of the partners complement each other rather than overlapping.

- *Common Values and Business Priorities*

In order for partners to cooperate effectively, they must have compatible values and beliefs. The degree of compatibility required varies according to the degree of involvement called for by the type of alliance. Because representatives from each of the partner companies will work together as part of the alliance, they should approach work from similar perspectives if the alliance is to be successful. For example, serious conflicts may arise if one organization is highly bureaucratic while the other one shuns policies and procedures. If the culture of one parent is highly competitive and the other stresses cooperation, managers from the two companies may find it difficult to work together.

Some styles and values are conducive to good alliances regardless of the rest of the company's culture. Two of the factors that generally contribute to effective partnerships between companies include flexibility, or the ability to change as conditions evolve, and ability to both learn from and teach the partner company.

Identifying Prospective Partners

In many cases, an alliance may result from the availability of an appropriate partner rather than from the pursuit of a formal strategy. In other cases, the need for an alliance may result in the search for an appropriate partner. In order to ensure that a partner or prospective partner is the ideal candidate for the alliance, the audit team should generate a long list of possible candidates. This list can be created by using a combination of the following tools:

- trade magazines (advertisements and editorial material)
- buyer's guides
- electronic (database) literature searching
- trade associations
- trade shows
- interviews with experts (both within and outside the initiating company)
- interviews with customers

Key customers and customer groups may also be good sources to suggest appropriate alliance partners. Names generated in this way may include firms that already supply services to customers, or that have done so in the past.

Screening Candidates against the Alliance Criteria

The initial list generated by the audit team can usually be trimmed without the expense of extensive research. In narrowing the list of candidates, audit team members may wish to eliminate companies that clearly do not offer capabilities or technologies that complement those of the initiating company. In general, good alliances will result when companies complement the strengths and weaknesses of their partners, rather than competing with them directly or offering similar contributions.

The screening process will continue for some time, and is usually an iterative process. Candidates are screened against the criteria repeatedly as more information is gathered, with the list of prospects continually revised until a few candidates who meet the criteria remain.

Research Partner Candidates

Initial research into partner qualifications can be done by using some of the same tools noted above in identifying candidate companies. The full gamut of primary and secondary market research tools can be accessed in this phase of alliance development. In addition, credit reports should be run on selected firms through Dun and Bradstreet or similar services.

The diagram in Figure 5 illustrates possible information sources and shows how they interlock to complete the profile of each partner candidate.

FIGURE 5
INFORMATION-GATHERING TOOLS FOR ALLIANCE DEVELOPMENT

Evaluation of the Final Candidates

Once the two or three most suitable partners have been identified, the following due diligence research should be completed. The result of this research should be compiled and assessed against the original criteria set out for the alliance, as well as the prospective partner's ability to work well with the initiating company.

Some of the following questions should be taken into account in evaluating the final candidates:

- Interview representatives from the prospective partner's customer base. How well does the company meet its customer needs? Have customers asked for the addition of service features that have been ignored or denied?

- How healthy are the prospective partners? Are they overly dependent on one customer? How stable is their financial performance?

- Do the candidates have a good reputation in its industry? Are they known for following through on their agreements, or do they pose risks that alliance partners would want to avoid? Do they have a service reputation that the initiating company would want to be linked to?

- Is there the potential for a good personal relationship between executives from the prospective partner companies? Do their goals for the alliance match up with the objectives of the initiating company?

- What other alliances are the partners or prospective partners involved in? How would this affect the alliance being audited?

Once good candidates have been identified and investigated through a variety of sources, they should be approached about their interest in developing an alliance. This is the next step to be described.

Step 4

INITIATE RELATIONSHIPS WITH SELECTED CANDIDATES

In cases where the executives of prospective partners are unknown by executives from the initiating firm, careful steps should be taken to set up an appropriate introduction of the two companies. This can be accomplished best through a party known by managers, executives or owners of both firms. The ability to use others known to both companies underscores the importance of using those knowledgeable about the industry in addition to printed sources to generate lists of prospective partners.

Where the potential alliance can provide significant benefit to specific customers, common customers can often introduce alliance candidates. If this is not possible, an excellent and very practical method of introduction is the use of a formal letter sent by the initiating firm to the candidate firm, giving background on the company and reasons for interest in a potential alliance. The letter should be followed up by a phone call to arrange a personal meeting.

Step 5

DEVELOP A RELATIONSHIP WITH PROSPECTIVE CANDIDATES

Because alliance relationships are often complex and intense, there are some aspects of a partnership that cannot be explored without actually developing a relationship between the partner companies. Once executives from the prospective partner companies have been introduced, representatives from the companies should engage in a courtship process to determine whether or not an alliance between their firms will be mutually beneficial. This process also helps to clarify what the formal terms of the alliance should include.

Issues to Address in the Courtship Process

In multiple conversations and meetings between potential alliance partners, some of the critical intangible issues that must be addressed are:

- Is this partner trustworthy?

- What are the readily apparent benefits of the alliance to each partner?

- How will the corporate cultures (ethics, operating style, objectives) of the alliance partners mesh or clash? Executives considering an alliance should put themselves in the shoes of the prospective partner and evaluate the benefits of the alliance to both sides. Only mutually beneficial alliances tend to succeed.

- Will the relationship be accepted by key executives, managers, and other employees of both partners?

- Will the relationship be accepted by key players in the industry or market?

- Have the details of the venture been sufficiently explained throughout the organization? Early disclosure is sometimes limited in publicly held companies by stock market considerations. Has information about the alliance been presented in enough detail to ensure that everyone sees the work that will be required in the future?

- Has a team structure been established to work together on the alliance? This team should include representatives from each of the partner companies who will be involved in the management of the venture resulting from the alliance. This ensures that the alliance will be planned in a way that will contribute to the achievement of its objectives.

- Has a joint business plan been prepared and realistically reviewed? The plan should be prepared by working teams from the partner companies. It should be reviewed by executives from the partner companies.

Establishing Personal Relationships

One of the critical elements of this phase of alliance development is the establishment of a one-on-one relationship between key individuals on both sides of the alliance. The people chosen to establish the alliance should possess the following skills and qualities:

- Cooperative
- Open and trustworthy
- Competent and helpful
- Friendly and social
- Fair and easy to work with
- Broad understanding of company operations
- Rational decision makers
- Respected by others inside and outside the company

When managers in Japanese companies are assigned to work on an alliance project, they are committed to working on the project for the life of the partnership. This allows a high level of trust to grow between the partner firms. Trust increases the life expectancy of the alliance, inasmuch as it increases the possibility of successfully revising the alliance to meet changing conditions that affect the partner companies.

Strong interpersonal linkages are critical to alliance success. General Electric gives its people responsible for managing strategic alliances the title of "corporate relations manager". While this strategy poses the risk of dependence on an individual or group of individuals, experience shows that the development of good personal relationships between representatives from the partner companies is much more important to the success of the venture than the terms of the formal agreement.

Step 6

EVALUATE THE FORMAL AGREEMENT

The key questions which need to be asked at this stage of alliance development should include:

- Can the contribution of each party be structured so as to avoid conflicts?
- Are there adequate exit provisions? If the alliance fails, what does each party retain? The annals of business are full of cases of companies who have left alliances and become major competitors. A good example is Microsoft, who originally supplied computer software development services to IBM to assist them in developing their disk operating system, and later became its primary competitor.
- Do both sides understand what each party is trying to achieve from the alliance? For example, some companies, including many Japanese firms, will enter an alliance with the sole purpose of learning new skills. Under these circumstances, the partner who enters the alliance with strictly commercial objectives may be sorely disappointed.
- Who will be the key competitors?
- Who is to do what, and by when, and what will happen if it is not done?
- If licensing or royalty agreements are involved, estimating the value of these agreements is difficult. Have the agreements been carefully defined, with consideration for guaranteed minimum, maximum royalties, audits, penalties if payments are delayed and taxation issues?
- Intellectual property rights are critical. Have they been clearly addressed?

Critical elements of the arrangement should be concluded before the formal agreement is written.

Executives should be careful if the only strong justification for the alliance is for one firm to expand its share of an industry, and for the other to boost a weak financial situation. Primerica recently invested $722.5 million in exchange for a 27 percent stake in Travelers Insurance. Travelers entered the alliance in part so that it could use the additional capital to make up for anticipated losses in its real estate and mortgage portfolios. Primerica borrowed the money to finance the purchase. It is too early to judge the other strategic benefits from this alliance, but such deals are usually fraught with peril.

Step 7

EVALUATE THE POST-AGREEMENT RELATIONSHIP

Perhaps the greatest challenge in managing an alliance effectively is to change it in a way that responds to the evolution of the conditions that affect it. An assessment of the following aspects of alliance management can help audit team members evaluate possible improvement strategies for an existing audit. It can also suggest safeguards that should be taken in the design of a new alliance.

Key Questions in Managing Alliances

The following questions address issues that consistently arise in the maintenance of service alliances.

- *Does the alliance have a clear identity? Do employees, customers and suppliers know who or what the alliance really is? Has this identity changed over time to address the changing needs of customers and other stakeholders?*

  Successful alliances require objectives that provide clear direction for their management teams. Clear goals result in the effective use of limited resources. A sense that the alliance is achieving the purpose for which it was designed can also be unifying force for the people involved in the alliance. With this sense of common purpose, managers participating in the alliance can direct their loyalties to the alliance, rather than thinking first and foremost of the priorities of the respective parent companies.

  One of the key characteristics of a good alliance is an ability to adjust over time. The ability of the partners to contribute and the comparative strength of the parent companies is bound to change over time. If the identity of the alliance does not change to correspond with these developments, the alliance will lose its ability to achieve its goals. The people involved in the alliance will not be united by a sense of common purpose, because the purpose they are charged with will be ineffective or irrelevant in the new situation.

- *Is there too much focus on internal alliance issues and not enough focus on the customer and competition?*

  This can be a general risk in all new businesses. If internal demands require constant attention, customer needs and intensifying competition may be overlooked. This problem can be avoided if care is taken to work out details of the venture in the planning stage. Inability to meet internal and external demands simultaneously may also indicate an insufficient allocation of resources or talent to the operation of the alliance.

- *Have the key marketing and sales issues been adequately addressed? How will the new service be sold?*

  In the end, an alliance with worthwhile goals and the most cooperative of management teams will be pointless if the services resulting from the alliances are not sold in a way that will make the venture financially rewarding. A significant part of the alliance planning process should include the development of a marketing strategy that is based on feedback from customers about their preferences and requirements. This marketing plan should be revisited with each audit cycle (usually every 18 to 24 months) to ensure that customers are still satisfied and to monitor their changing demands.

Long-Term Issues in Alliance Management

The average life expectancy of a strategic alliance is seven years. Some alliances end in acquisition, usually by one of the parents. Others fail and are disbanded by the partners. Still others are designed to be temporary, and are systematically ended when their objectives have been accomplished.

In many cases, however, alliances end because they do not change to meet evolving needs. Attending to the following issues can help managers assess the performance of an alliance in terms of its ability to meet new demands. An audit of these issues can also point to opportunities for improvement in the operation of the alliance. The description of the importance of each issue is followed by questions for evaluating the performance (or potential) of an alliance for each issue.

Balance between the Partners

Like all business functions, alliances should go through continuous improvements and progressive stages. Managers must adapt to change, which is impossible if the relationship is rigid. Partners must also make sure that the alliance does not "hollow out" or "deskill" either company, permitting internal skill sets to deteriorate through inappropriate division of labor. This usually happens when there is an unequal commitment to the alliance by the partners involved, or when one company brings significantly more to the relationship than its partner does.

A recent study by McKinsey and Company revealed an interesting point about successful alliances. The study concluded that alliances usually work best when ownership of the new venture is shared equally. This contradicts the conventional wisdom used by US and European managers that one company must play a dominant role, having a minimum of 51 percent ownership.[6] The fact that 50-50 ownership works best in alliances underscores an important feature of alliances, as compared to acquisitions or other forms of management agreements. Companies that are engaged in strategic alliances must abandon the traditional competitive mentality and learn to manage with less control than in the past. Equally shared ownership helps to foster this attitude.

- Is ownership of the alliance equally shared?

- Do the partners make equal contributions or trades in terms of money, resources, people, technology, skill, and access to markets?

- Is the alliance evaluated on a regular basis to ensure that changes in the strengths and interests of each of the partners is reflected in the ownership arrangement?

Ability to Learn from Alliance Partners

Partners must be able to learn from each other in order to allow the alliance to grow. Every company has a different way of doing things. Strategic alliances offer the opportunity to observe how another company operates — the way customers are served, how new business is developed, how internal management works. Once people participating in the alliance have learned new skills from the partner company, this learning can be shared and integrated with others in the parent company. Managers in the alliance should also embrace the ideas of the partner company in managing the alliance.

- Is the initiating company willing to integrate ideas learned from the other partner in the management of the alliance?

- Is the initiating company willing to offer management ideas that will improve the performance of the alliance?

- Are the partners willing to integrate ideas from other companies in the management of the alliance?

- Are the partners willing to offer management ideas that will improve the performance of the alliance?

Cultural Compatibility

Cultural conflicts are bound to occur with even the most carefully chosen alliance partners. Conflict can arise in a number of different ways. Differences in company management styles is one of the major causes of difficulty in strategic alliances. These differences occur not only across national boundaries, but within countries as well. For example, large companies tend to have more policies and procedures than small companies do. Large company managers may see small company managers as not playing according to the rules, while small company managers may feel that representatives from large companies are bogged down in bureaucracy.

Although companies should seek partners with appropriate cultural characteristics, bridging cultural gaps requires understanding and forbearance, even when culture has been taken into consideration when seeking a partner. It is important that all members of the partnership team know what is involved. They should know how their partner makes decisions and where the limits of authority lie. They must also try to understand a partner's procedures for planning and measuring performance, and its rules for social and business behavior.

- What are the similarities and differences between the culture of the initiating company and those of its current or prospective alliance partners?

- How will these differences affect the business of the particular alliance?

- Have mechanisms been discussed for resolving cultural differences that arise in the management of the alliance?

SUMMARY

The need to constantly innovate in order to meet the demands of a competitive environment has never been greater. No company will be able to meet all of the demands for services required by its customer base. Strategic alliances will become an ever more important tool for increasing service offering and service quality in the coming years. This is because alliances allow companies to meet market demands more quickly and with an investment of fewer resources.

At the same time, an increasing reliance on alliances between companies will force managers to think in new ways. This will require a willingness to cooperate with and trust those who have been seen as threatening competitors in the past. It will also require managers to operate with less control than they have had in the past. Maintaining this sort of relationship will require the commitment of more time and resources than wholly owned operations. Because of the investment required, alliance partners should take measures to insure that joint ventures operate as effectively as possible, thereby producing optimal dividends.

This audit guide has outlined a number of areas where alliance performance can be improved. Repetition of the audit on a regular cycle will measure improvements in alliance performance and point to changes that can be made to accommodate conditions that have evolved.

References

1 Kathryn Rudie Harrigan, "Strategic Alliances and Partner Asymmetries," in *Cooperative Strategies in International Business*, edited by Farok J. Contractor and Peter Lorange, Lexington Books, 1988.

2 Joel Bleeke and David Ernst, "The Way to Win in Cross-Border Alliances," in *Collaborating to Compete,* edited by Joel Bleeke and David Ernst, John Wiley and Sons, 1993, p. 28.

3 Joseph B. Fuller, James O'Conor and Richard Rawlinson, "Tailored Logistics: The Next Advantage," *Harvard Business Review*, May-June 1993.

4 Beth McGoldrick, "Joint Ventures: Creating an Identity Crisis," *Corporate Finance*, May 1993.

5 Peter Lorange, Johan Roos and Peggy Bronn, "Building Successful Strategic Alliances," *Long Range Planning*, 1992.

6 Joel Bleek and David Ernst, "The Death of the Predator," in *Collaborating to Compete: Using Strategic Alliances and Acquisitions in the Global Marketplace*, John Wiley and Sons, 1993, pp. 1-16.

7 Varun Bery and Thomas A. Bowers, "Rebuilding an Alliance," in *Collaborating to Compete*, ed. by Joel Bleeke and David Ernst, John Wiley and Sons, 1993, pp. 67-78.

Part 3

THE AUDIT PROCESS

This section addresses the logistical and process requirements of conducting an audit. The topics covered in this section include:

- Staffing the audit team
- Creating an audit project plan
- Laying the groundwork for the audit
- Analyzing audit results
- Sharing audit results
- Writing effective audit reports
- Dealing with resistance to audit recommendations
- Building an ongoing audit program

STAFFING THE AUDIT TEAM

Who conducts the audit is as important in many ways as how the audit is conducted. In fact, the people selected for the audit team will, in large part, determine how the audit is done, how results are analyzed, and how findings are reported. The following list includes general characteristics of effective audit teams for most areas:

- Consists of three to four people.
- Reports to CEO or other senior executive.
- Represents a carefully selected range of skills and experience.

More than four people may be needed for an audit team if data gathering is labor intensive, as when large numbers of customers or employees must be interviewed. However, audit teams of more than six or seven people present problems of maintaining uniformity and communicating audit progress and findings during the course of the evaluation.

Selecting an Audit Team Leader

The audit team leader will play a strong role in shaping both the data gathering and the findings from the audit. The strength of the team leader will also influence the acceptance of the audit, both in terms of enlisting cooperation in the data gathering phase and in securing support for improvement initiatives that grow out of the audit. Because of the importance of this role, care should be taken in selecting the appropriate person for the job. The following qualities are found in successful audit team leaders:

- Has a good relationship with the CEO or with the executive-level sponsor of the audit.
- Is well-liked and well-respected at all levels of the organization, especially in the area to be audited.
- Has good interpersonal skills; can maintain good relationships even in difficult circumstances.
- Has good analytical skills; can assimilate and process large amounts of complex data quickly.

- Has some knowledge of the function or area being audited.
- Has extensive knowledge of the type of process being audited.
- Communicates ideas clearly and effectively.

Skills to Be Represented on the Audit Team

Once the team leader has been chosen, audit team members should be selected on the basis of what each can bring to the project. Selection efforts should focus on developing a balanced representation of the following qualities:

- A variety of tenures in the organization, with relative newcomers preferably having experience in other organizations.
- A variety of familiarity with the area (function or site) being audited. Those who are intimately familiar with the area can serve as guides to the less familiar; those who are new to the area can provide objectivity and ask questions that might never be considered by those more involved in the area.
- Considerable familiarity with the type of process being audited. For this reason, many organizations call on people filling roles in similar processes from other parts of the company to work on audit teams.
- Good analytical skills.
- Good interpersonal skills.
- Good facilitation and interviewing skills.
- Good communication skills.
- An understanding of the company's strategy and direction.

CREATING AN AUDIT PROJECT PLAN

Creating an audit project plan accomplishes the following objectives:

- Ensures the allocation of adequate resources, or helps audit team members be prepared to improvise in the face of short resources.

- Ensures the audit is timed so resources are available that may be in high demand.

- Creates clear expectations in the minds of team members about what must be done, and when — especially important when they are not committed to the project full-time.

- Ensures accountability for what must be done, who is responsible for which tasks, and when the audit must be completed.

Financial audits often rely on the Critical Path Method (CPM) of project planning. This method was originally developed by the US Department of Defense during World War II to facilitate the timely completion of weapons development and production. It has since been modified to plan a wide variety of projects. The following outline is a simplification of CPM. It suggests the aspects of a project that should be taken into account during the planning phase.

Critical Path Method

In developing the project plan, audit team members should ask and answer the following questions:

- *What tasks must be performed?*

This list should include the major tasks outlined in the audits, along with subtasks that grow out of those major headings. It should also include any tasks mandated by unique circumstances in the company performing the self-assessment. The audit team may want to brainstorm about tasks that need to be performed, then refine the list to reflect the work priorities of the audit.

- *In what order will the tasks be completed?*

Answering this question should include an analysis of which tasks and sub tasks are dependent on others. Which tasks cannot begin until another has been completed?

Which tasks can be done at any time? The audit team may want to place the ordered task on a time line, with start dates, expected duration of the step, and end dates outlined for each task.

- *Who will perform each task?*

Most tasks will be performed by members of the audit team. These assignments should be made by taking the strengths of each team member into consideration, as well as the time availability of each person. Equity of work load should also be taken into account. If tasks are to be assigned to people not on the audit team, those individuals should be included or consulted at this point.

- *What resources will be needed for each step?*

Each task should be analyzed in terms of the personnel, budget, equipment, facilities, support services, and any other resources that will be needed for its completion. The team should assess the availability of all of the resources. Consideration should be given to the task ordering completed earlier. Are some resources subject to competing demands, and therefore difficult to secure at a particular time? How far in advance do arrangements for resources need to be made? Does the task order or time line need to be revised in light of what is known about resource availability?

- *Where is the slack time?*

Slack time is unscheduled time between dependent tasks. Slack provides a degree of flexibility in altering the start dates of subsequent tasks. Slack time signals that a task has a range of possible start dates. It is used to determine the critical path.

- *What is the critical path?*

The critical path in a project is the set of tasks that must be completed in a sequential, chronological order. If any task on the critical path is not completed, all subsequent tasks will be delayed. Delays at any point in the critical path will result in an equivalent delay in the completion of the total project.

Regardless of the method used to develop the project plan, no project, regardless how simple, is ever completed in exact accordance with its plan. However, having a project plan allows the team to gauge its progress, anticipate problems and determine where alternative approaches are needed.

LAYING THE GROUNDWORK FOR THE AUDIT

Once the team has been selected and a project plan developed, the audit leader should prepare those who will be involved in and affected by the audit for the team's visit or for data-gathering. The following steps will help the audit to run more smoothly:

Communicate Executive Support for the Audit

Demonstrating executive support for the audit accomplishes two goals. First, it increases the chances that those involved in the area being audited will cooperate with data gathering efforts. Second, it shows executive support for the area being audited and suggests a commitment to improving the area's performance.

In many companies, the audit is introduced by the executive sponsor of the audit by means of a memo. The memo should explain the purpose of the audit and ask for the support of everyone in the area being audited. This memo is distributed to everyone within the company who will be affected by or involved in the data gathering process. The most effective memos explain how the audit results will be used, reassuring those who will be responding to audit team requests about the motives of the audit. The credibility of such memos is also bolstered when previous audits have been acted upon with positive results.

Make Arrangements with the Area to Be Audited

The audit team leader should check with the appropriate manager in charge of the process or site being audited to arrange for any required on-site visits, interviewing, surveys, focus groups, or written information needed for the audit. The team leader should also explain the purpose, scope, and expected duration of the audit; review the project plan with the manager; and answer any questions the manager has about the audit.

The team leader should also work with the appropriate manager or managers to determine how the audit can be conducted with the least impact on the flow of work. This may include discussions about the timing of the audit, the options for data gathering, the availability of needed data, and possibilities for generating the necessary information quickly and easily. Finding ways to make data collection more efficient and effective is especially important when the audit is part of an ongoing program, rather than an isolated assessment.

Develop a Protocol or Checklist

A protocol or checklist can be used by the audit team to outline the issues that are central to the audit. Written guides can help the leaders of those areas being audited to prepare for the audit. A protocol represents a plan of what the audit team will do to accomplish the objectives of the audit. It is an important tool of the audit, since it not only serves as the audit team's guide to collecting data, but also as a record of the audit procedures completed by the team. In some cases, audit teams may even want to format the checklist in a way that allows them to record their field notes directly on the checklist.

The checklist should include no more than twenty major items, and checklists should be updated with each audit in order to ensure that the appropriate measures are taken. Items where improvement initiatives have been successful should be eliminated from the checklist, with newly identified possibilities for improvement opportunities added.

ANALYZING AUDIT RESULTS

Discovering gaps between a company's targets and its actual performance is a relatively easy task. Tools are provided to assist audit teams in assessing their performance in a given area. In most cases, more opportunities for improvement will be uncovered by an audit than can be addressed by the resources and energy available. Therefore, one of the most difficult aspects of analyzing the results of an audit lies in determining which opportunities are the most important for managers to pursue.

Because resources and energy for pursuing improvement initiatives are limited, choices must be made about which options are most important. Sometimes these decisions are based on political winds in the company, or on what has worked well in the past, or on personal preferences of top management. However, scarce resources will be used more effectively if allocated to the areas where they will have the greatest impact. Managers must also determine the most effective way to approach initiatives. This section discusses criteria for prioritizing opportunities that grow out of audit findings.

The Novations Strategic Alignment Model

The mid-1980s saw the birth of the "excellence" movement, where many companies tried to achieve excellence in every area of endeavour. Although the movement created an awareness of the need for management improvements, it failed to consider that not all management processes are equal in terms of producing benefits. As a result, leading organizations in today's environment focus on performing well in a few core areas. Knowing what those core areas are depends on a clear vision of the company's strategy.

Strategic thinking about which areas should be improved involves much more than taking an inventory of current capabilities and weaknesses. If it did not, existing capabilities would always determine strategic objectives, and organizational growth and development would come to a halt. To set priorities strategically, companies must decide which improvement opportunities fall in the following categories:

- What to do themselves.
- What to do with someone else.
- What to contract others to do.
- What not to do.

FIGURE 1
CATEGORIES OF WORK

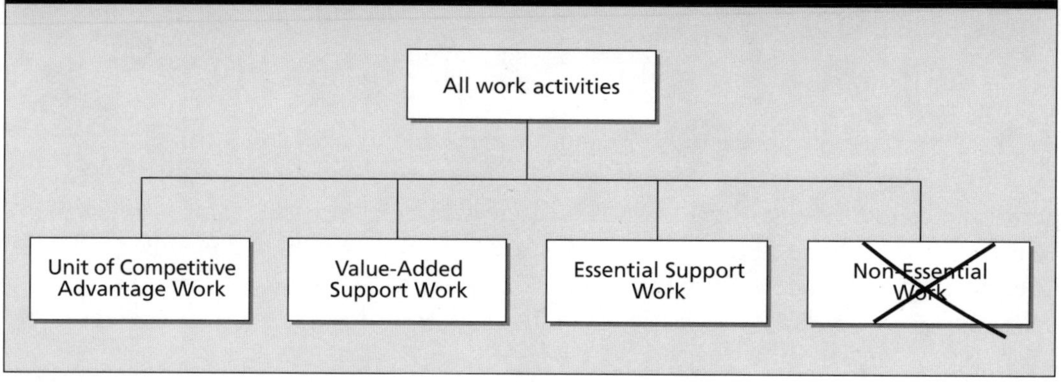

Figure 1 illustrates the four categories of work.

Unit of Competitive Advantage (UCA) Work includes work and capabilities that create distinctiveness for the business in the marketplace.

Value-added Support Work facilitates the accomplishment of the UCA work. For example, a company may have a technology orientation rather than a service orientation, but an effective logistics process may help them to improve their UCA work of providing cutting edge technology.

Essential Support Work neither creates advantage nor facilitates the work that creates advantage, but must be done if businesses are to continue to operate (includes such things as paying taxes, maintaining payroll records, etc.).

Nonessential Work is activity that has lost its usefulness but continues to be done because of tradition.

Despite their sophistication in dealing with other aspects of business, most managers have archaic views of the different types of work. Many of their models for characterizing work have come from a finance or accounting orientation. Accounting terms such as overhead, direct labor, and indirect labor may be useful as a way to report costs, but they provide little understanding about the relative strategic importance of the work. Yet these classifications are frequently used to determine how work is organized and where resources are allocated.

The concept of *unit of competitive advantage* (UCA) helps to explain why some organizations either emphasize the wrong capabilities or de-emphasize the right capabilities. UCA also explains why some forms of improvement lead to competitive disadvantage, and why some businesses consistently outperform their competitors by gaining greater leverage from their competitive advantages.

A company's UCA includes the critical processes that create distinctiveness within an established strategic direction. It is based on the premise that businesses create competitive advantage when they focus their attention on a few key processes and implement those key processes in world-class fashion. For example, continuous improvement is a popular management program that assumes benefit from any kind of ongoing improvement. Generally speaking, however, continuous improvement program will only create competitive advantage when an organization defines a strategic direction, clarifies strategic objectives, and determines its UCA. These crucial prerequisites tell where continuous improvement efforts should be focused to create maximum leverage. They suggest what kinds of work to improve interdependently, what kinds to improve separately, and what kinds not to waste time on. They even signal when continuous improvement is more likely to create competitive disadvantage rather than competitive advantage.

UCA Initiatives Should Take Priority

Understanding what work falls under which categories requires a clear understanding of the company's strategy. The initiatives resulting from an audit that affect the Unit of Competitive Advantage work processes should clearly have the highest priority among improvement projects. Value-added support initiatives should be second priority, and essential support work should be the third priority. Nonessential work should not be continued.

Once improvement opportunities that will have the greatest impact on the achievement of the company's goals have been identified, the following ideas can be used to lend further insight into how opportunities identified through an audit should be prioritized:

- *Focus on the two or three most important areas.*

Insisting that action be taken on all of the problems uncovered by the audit may overwhelm the people who are responsible for bringing about those changes. Flatter organizations and leaner work forces mean that people are already being asked to do more work with fewer resources and less time. Producing a long list of improvement initiatives may prompt people to dismiss all of them because they don't have time to complete the whole list.

- *Focus on the areas that can be changed.*

Emphasizing problems that are beyond the control of the people who are responsible to work on process improvement only leads to cynicism and a sense of powerlessness. By focusing on things that are within the sphere of influence, accountability for each part of the action plan can be clearly defined.

• *Include as priorities some improvements that can be made quickly.*

Rapid, visible improvement helps build support for more complicated initiatives. Quick improvements also reassure people of management's support for long-term improvement. Seeing immediate improvement helps to build commitment at all levels to the process, and helps build momentum for further change.

• *Emphasize the improvements that seem essential to long-term success.*

Essential improvements may involve sensitive issues or difficult problems, such as deficiencies in fundamental skill levels within the organization or basic strategy issues. These problems are not only difficult and expensive to address, but may also cause a great deal of personal pain or require significant individual adjustment. Nevertheless, long-term improvement requires a commitment to dealing with difficult issues rather than avoiding them.

SHARING AUDIT RESULTS

In most cases, audit results will be presented to various interested people in a feedback meeting. Those in attendance may include members of the executive team, managers who work in the area covered by the audit, the audit team members, and anyone else who is affected by or interested in the results. The meeting should be conducted by members of the audit team. The purpose is to present their findings, and make recommendations for capitalizing on opportunities for improvement.

Conducting Effective Feedback Meetings

The audit team's strategy for the meeting should be to present a clear and simple picture of the current situation as revealed by the audit. This may be a moment of truth for those who have been anticipating the audit results. The feedback meeting for an audit holds both excitement and anxiety: excitement that the future will be bright, and anxiety that shortcomings in individual performance will be highlighted and demands made for personal change. As a result, the meeting must be carefully managed in order to lead to productive change. The following structure is one recommended format for conducting a feedback meeting.

- *Introduce the meeting and preview its agenda.*

This might include an overview of the original intent of the audit, introduction of the audit team, and a brief summary of the meeting's agenda. This step should take no more than five minutes.

- *Present the audit findings.*

Audit findings should summarize the most important points revealed by the data gathered in the audit process. They should be presented separately from the audit recommendations in order to allow people to digest the two parts of the presentation separately. Clearing up misunderstandings about the findings may make the group more accepting of the team's recommendations.

The presentation of the audit findings should take comparatively little time. Audits almost always generate much more data than can be effectively presented or digested in a feedback meeting. The goal of the audit team should be to zero in on the two or three most important points learned from the audit, and present enough supporting data to illustrate those points.

Presenting too much data about audit findings has a number of negative effects. It encourages people to conduct their own analysis of the audit data. To a certain extent, this is a healthy and normal reaction. If others understand the evidence that supports the conclusions drawn by the audit team, they are more likely to accept and own the audit results. Therefore, they will be more committed to the changes brought about by the audit results. However, when people immerse themselves in large amounts of data, they may become victims of "analysis paralysis": they may spend unnecessary time attempting to explain contradictory data, or trying to understand methods used by others to gather data.

• *Present audit recommendations.*

Presenting the audit recommendations should be the central point of the meeting. The recommendations should grow out of the data highlights presented. The audit team should view the recommendations as discussion points for the meeting, rather than as absolute action items.

A common mistake in feedback meetings is to spend most of the meeting on presenting data and recommendations. It is easy for audit team members to become enamored of data they have invested considerable time and energy to collect and analyze. Others in the audience will probably also be interested in the details of the data collected. However, if too much time is spent on discussing the recommendations, the meeting will end before a commitment to action has been made.

• *Ask others to react to the data.*

The reactions of top management and those responsible for implementing audit recommendations will determine the ultimate value of the audit data. Therefore, the feedback meeting is a good time to resolve questions or problems with the findings and recommendations as they have been presented. If resistance to the audit findings is not resolved in the feedback meeting, opportunities for improvement may be lost.

Those attending the meeting may offer their opinions willingly. If not, the audit team members should ask the others in the room for their reaction to what has been presented.

• *Develop preliminary action plans.*

The detailed action plans should grow out of the recommendations made by the audit team. They should specifically address the question of who should do what by when. Formal accountability mechanisms should be established before the end of the meeting, such as the scheduling of subsequent meetings or follow-up check points.

WRITING EFFECTIVE AUDIT REPORTS

There are three fundamental purposes for writing a formal report at the conclusion of an audit:

- An audit report may be a stand-alone summary of the audit. This approach is not recommended, inasmuch as the report is likely to be filed away, making the probability of action unlikely.

- The report may supplement a feedback meeting, providing those in attendance with documentation and an outline to follow.

- The report should also serve as a baseline document to make measurement of performance improvement possible in future audits.

Because the written report is the most enduring part of the audit presentation, it should be well written and easy to understand. The following tips will lead to the preparation of effective written audit reports.

Focus on a Few Key Points

The audit presentation should focus on the two or three most important findings. It is impossible to present all of the data gathered in the audit to those who were not on the audit team. It is also not advisable to present every detail of the data. The audit team members should trust their own judgment about what the highlights of the study were, and present enough data to support that judgment. For each of the major findings, the team may want to include the following information:

- What is the problem?

- Why does it exist?

- What happens if the problem is not fixed:
  — in the short term?
  — in the long term?

- Recommend solutions.

- Outline expected benefits.

Prepare an Outline Before Writing the First Draft

A good outline ensures that the logic of the report is clear, and that ideas proceed in an order that makes sense. The following outline provides one approach that works effectively.

Background

This section should establish the framework for the audit in terms of:

- Providing a brief discussion of the overall purpose of the audit.
- Identifying the role of the audit team in the overall process.
- Establishing the limitations of the audit methodology to ensure that others utilize the results provided in the report appropriately.

Objectives

This section should identify specific objectives of the audit in terms of types of information the team was expected to generate.

Methodology

The methodology section should describe the mechanics of the audit and include the following information:

- Types of assessment used (survey, interviews, focus groups, etc.).
- Data sources, or the sample groups for each of the types of assessment used.
- Time frame during which the audit was conducted.
- Other pertinent details about how the audit was conducted.

Findings

This section is designed to provide others with a review of the "facts" that came out of the audit. Except in cases where an audit checks regulatory compliance, only the most significant findings should be discussed in any detail in the report. This section should also include briefly presented data supporting the findings.

Conclusions

This section should report the audit team's interpretation of what the facts of the audit mean in light of the objectives stated at the outset of the audit.

Recommendations

This section includes suggestions from the audit team on how to close the performance gaps identified in the audit. The degree of specificity to be included in the audit report will vary from company to company and audit to audit.

Appendix

This portion of the formal report should include any of the following items that are relevant to the audit:

- A copy of any questionnaires or survey instruments used in the audit.
- A summary of the data gathered in the course of the audit.
- Recommendations for subsequent audits based on the team's experience.

Present Audit Findings Accurately

Those who read the report will no doubt be somewhat familiar with the area covered by the audit. They may notice discrepancies between what they know about the subject and what is reported in the written document. Spotting one inaccuracy may lead the readers to discredit all of the findings, conclusions and recommendations. Audit team members should be careful to report data as it was actually generated, and to describe the impact of the findings accurately.

Use Clear, Concise Language

Every statement included in the report should be based on sound evidence developed or reviewed during the audit. Whatever is said must be supported or supportable. Speculation should be avoided. Generalities and vague reporting will only confuse and mislead those that the report should influence or inform. For example, a report using the terms *some*, *a few*, or *not all* can leave the reader confused about the significance of the finding. Specific quantities should be used, such as, "of the ten samples taken, two were found to be…", "Three of five respondents said that…", and so on. Statements should be qualified as needed, and any unconfirmed data or information should be identified as such.

Ideas or sentences that do not amplify the central theme should be eliminated. The report should not identify individuals or highlight the mistakes of individuals.

Use Good Grammar and Style

Basic grammar and style rules should be followed in writing the text. Below are some examples:

- Avoid extreme terms, such as alarming, deplorable, gross negligence, etc.
- Avoid using redundant or lengthy phrases, such as calling something an emergency situation when the word emergency alone will do.
- Avoid verbs camouflaged as nouns or adjectives. For example, use "the new procedure will reduce error entries," rather than "The new procedure will accomplish a reduction of error entries."
- Avoid indirect expressions where possible. For example, "Many instances of poor management were found," is more direct than saying, "There were many instances of poor judgment found."
- Use short, familiar words. Use words that are easily understandable to everyone and that convey the message concisely.
- Keep sentences short. Most writing experts suggest that an average sentence should be between 15 and 18 words. Packing too many ideas into a single sentence confuses and tires readers.

The audit team should provide enough background information in the report so that the reader clearly understands who conducted the audit and what the audit did or did not include. The purpose of the report as well as the purpose and scope of the audit should also be described in a manner that enables the reader to know why the report was written and who should take corrective action.

Timing of the Report

The timing of audit reports is critical to the overall reporting process and must be carefully thought out. In many cases, a written draft of the audit report is prepared one to three weeks before the feedback meeting. This draft then goes through a review and another report is prepared in time for the team's presentation. A final report may be completed after the feedback session has been held in order to record changes resulting from that meeting.

DEALING WITH RESISTANCE TO RECOMMENDATIONS

Most audit teams feel that if they can present their ideas clearly and logically, and have the best interests of the company or department at heart, managers will accept the recommendations made as part of the audit and follow the team's recommendations. Many people who have worked in organizations, however, find that no matter how reasonably recommendations are presented, they are all too often not implemented.

Implementation usually fails because it requires people to change their ways of working. That change requires a great deal of effort, energy, and risk; therefore, change is usually resisted. Resistance is an emotional process; people may embrace recommendations based on their logic, but fail to implement them because of the emotional resistance to the personal change involved. Resistance is a predictable, natural, and necessary part of the learning process. Although resistance may cause audit team members to feel they have missed the mark in terms of the recommendations they have made, it actually often signals accuracy in having interpreted the organization's needs. By dealing with the resistance directly, audit teams can work through barriers to implementing process improvements.

What Are the Signs of Resistance?

In many cases, resistance may be expressed directly. Direct objections to recommendations are relatively easy to address, inasmuch as they can be discussed and resolved. When recommendations are being presented, team members should stop frequently to allow those who are listening to the report to voice any objections or disagreements. Those who are presenting the data should be careful not to become defensive or to punish those who express reservations about the recommendations. It is impossible to deal with objections unless they are voiced; therefore, the audit team should welcome the expression of objections or differences of opinion. The following tips may be used for surfacing and dealing with direct resistance:

- Provide many opportunities for others to express their concerns.

- Carefully clarify any confusing concerns.

- Deal with important or easy concerns immediately. Defer the remainder.

- Summarize the concerns before moving on. Show that concerns have been heard.

- It may even be helpful to list concerns on a flip chart or blackboard.

If direct resistance continues, the following steps may be necessary:

- Talk about the differences of opinion.
- Voice concern and support for negotiating a resolution.
- Avoid struggles for control of the situation.

Dealing with Indirect Resistance

In other cases, resistance may be subtle and elusive. Indirect resistance is difficult to identify and deal with because its manifestations seem logical. People who are experiencing indirect resistance may feel that they are "getting the run around." Many different forms of resistance may manifest themselves in a single meeting:

- Request for more detail.
- Providing too much detail in response to questions.
- Complaining that there isn't enough time to implement recommendations.
- Claiming that the recommendations are impractical.
- Attacking those who propose improvement initiatives.
- Acting confused.
- Responding with silence.
- Intellectualizing about the data.
- Moralizing that problems wouldn't exist if it weren't for "those people".
- Agreeing to implement recommendations with no intention of acting on them.
- Asking questions about methodology.
- Arguing that previous problems have resolved themselves.
- Focusing on solutions before findings are fully understood.

Almost any of these responses is legitimate in moderate amounts. For example, members of the group may have concerns about the audit's methodology that should be considered. Managers may realistically wonder where they will find the time to implement recommendations. However, if refusal to act on recommendations persists once legitimate concerns have been addressed, then the audit team is probably facing indirect resistance.

Many models used in sales training provide recommendations for overcoming resistance. These methods suggest the use of data and logical arguments to win the point and convince the other person to buy whatever is being sold. These models work well for direct resistance. However, indirect resistance is normally based on feelings rather than logic. Therefore, the only way to truly overcome resistance is to deal with the emotional processes that cause it to happen in the first place. It is almost impossible to talk people out of the way they feel.

Feelings pass and change when they are expressed directly. A key skill for audit teams that are attempting to implement recommendations is to ask the people who are presenting resistance to put directly into words what they are experiencing. The most effective way to make this happen is for the audit team members to address directly what is happening in the situation. The following keys provide help in surfacing and dealing with indirect resistance.

- *Work once or twice with the person's concern, even when it feels as if he or she is resisting recommendations.*

By attempting to work with the problem stated by the person raising a concern, audit team members can determine whether the concern is legitimate or whether it is an excuse for not taking action. If the issues raised are legitimate, the person should show some willingness to discuss and resolve them. If the issues are manifestations of indirect resistance, the person will probably respond with other forms of resistance.

- *Identify the form the resistance is taking.*

Paying attention to the dynamics of a discussion can provide important clues as to whether or not a person is resisting recommendations. If a person is consistently distancing him or herself from those who are presenting the audit findings, using gestures or postures that suggest tension or discomfort, while at the same time presenting arguments for why the recommendations presented are inappropriate, it is probably a sign of resistance. The non-verbal responses of the presenters may also signal the onset of resistance. If presenters feel that they are suppressing negative feelings or becoming bored or irritated, it may be further evidence that the client is resisting.

Once presenters become aware of the resistance, the next step is to put it into words. This is best done by using neutral, everyday language. The skill is to describe the form of the resistance in a way that encourages the person to make a more direct statement of the reservation he or she is experiencing.

One general rule for stating what type of resistance is being manifested is to phrase the statement in common, non-threatening language. Statements should be made in the same tone and language that would be used to address a problem with a spouse or close friend. The statement should be made with as little evaluation as possible; it is the presenter's observation about what is happening in the situation.

A second general rule for surfacing indirect resistance involves not talking for a couple of moments after the presenter has stated what he or she has observed. There may be a temptation to elaborate on the observation, or to support it with evidence. However, continuing the statement will reduce the tension in the situation. Without tension, the person who is resisting feels no discomfort, and is unlikely to address the issue directly. Moreover, elaborating on the original statement may increase the other person's defensiveness and reduce the chances of solving the problem.

If stating the problem in direct, non-punishing terms fails to bring the resistance out into the open, there may be little more the audit team can do to overcome the indirect resistance. The best strategy in this case is to avoid resisting the resistance. Team members should support the person who is resisting and proceed with the implementation of recommendations to the extent possible.

BUILDING AN ONGOING AUDIT PROGRAM

As the pace of change increases, and as organization leaders become more and more committed to continuously improving their effectiveness and efficiency, audits of all types of processes will become more common. The most effective companies will establish program of ongoing audits, whereby a number of goals can be accomplished:

- Performance improvements can be measured over time.
- Important changes in the company's environment can be systematically monitored.
- Managers can make a habit of change and improvement, rather than resisting it.
- Those areas that are of highest importance to the company can be routinely improved.
- Processes can be modified to be in alignment with changes in strategy or in the environment.

As with all management techniques, however, an enduring program of ongoing audits requires that audits become integrated into the overall management system. The following guidelines are keys to weaving audits into the fabric of day-to-day operations.

Establish Support for Ongoing Audits

While support for audits begins at the executive level, ownership for the audit process must be felt throughout the organization if an ongoing program is to be successful. The following actions will help to broaden support for the audit process, while ensuring greater benefit from the audit.

- *Share the results of the audit with everyone throughout the organization.*

By keeping others informed about the results of an audit, managers reassure those who participate in and are affected by the audit of the integrity of the process. Employees sometimes become suspicious of probing investigators; they may have doubts about how the information will be used, or whether the information will be used. By sharing audit results, managers make an implicit commitment to improving the processes that have been evaluated.

- *Act on the audit results.*

Questions will be raised about continuing audits if early assessments bear no fruits. Failing to act on performance gaps that are identified leads to cynicism and lack of trust among those who work with the problems daily. On the other hand, improving a process can create the momentum that comes from accomplishment. Committing resources and attention to the improvement opportunities revealed by an audit also shows management commitment to the improvement process.

- *Let others know when performance has improved.*

Communicating the positive results from an audit is one way of rewarding the people who contributed to that improvement. It also builds faith in the effectiveness of the audit process. Moreover, showing that performance has improved is another means of reassuring people of a commitment to the improvement process.

- *Reward people for their part in improvements.*

Increasing efficiency and effectiveness can often be a threatening experience for those who are involved in a work process. Improving the way resources are used often means eliminating the need for some of the people who have been involved in the process. Although flatter, leaner organizations often preclude the possibility of offering promotions, managers should nevertheless attempt to ensure that people who contribute to performance improvement find their own situations better rather than worse as a result.

Rewards for helping to close performance gaps may span a range from thanking people for their efforts to planning a group celebration to offering bonuses or pay increases for improvement. Rewards are especially meaningful when people are allowed to suggest what rewards they would like for their contribution. This may provide managers with new ideas for rewards that may be less costly to the organization than financial recognition.

- *Involve a wide variety of people in the audit process.*

People can be involved in the audit process in many ways. By involving people from a broad spectrum, more people learn about audit techniques and results, thus spreading commitment to the audit process throughout the organization. By involving many people in the data-gathering process, employees feel that action plans growing out of the audit were a result of their input. Excluding people from the data-gathering phase usually reduces the feeling of ownership for the results, thus making people feel as if initiatives are being imposed on them. By the same token, involving a broad range of people in the development of action plans expands ownership for the plans and allows for the generation of more ideas.

Part 4

IMPLEMENTING A PARTNERSHIP AND ALLIANCES AUDIT: QUESTIONS AND CHECKLISTS

This section of the Partnership and Alliances Audit comprises a series of questions based on the six steps given in *Steps in Conducting a Strategic Alliance Audit – Manufacturing* (Part 1: The Strategic Alliance Audit for Manufacturing Firms), and the seven steps given in *Steps in Conducting a Strategic Alliance Audit – Services* (Part 2: The Strategic Alliance Audit for Service Firms).

These questions have been designed to help you plan and implement your audit in a straightforward and practical manner, covering all the relevant parts of the audit in the correct sequence. Additionally, background information is given for each step before the questions themselves are listed.

Part 1: The Strategic Alliance Audit for Manufacturing Firms

STEPS IN CONDUCTING A STRATEGIC ALLIANCE AUDIT (MANUFACTURING)

- Step 1 Clarify the Objectives of the Alliance
- Step 2 Evaluate the Plan for the Alliance
- Step 3 Specify Partner Criteria
- Step 4 Screen and Investigate Partners
- Step 5 Assess the Alliance Agreement
- Step 6 Evaluate the Ability of the Alliance to Meet Changing Conditions

Part 2: The Strategic Alliance Audit for Service Firms

STEPS IN CONDUCTING A STRATEGIC ALLIANCE AUDIT (SERVICES)

- Step 1 Determine the Appropriate Type of Alliance
- Step 2 Determine Customer Requirements and Establish Audit Criteria
- Step 3 Evaluate Suitability of Current or Potential Partners
- Step 4 Initiate Relationships with Selected Candidates
- Step 5 Develop a Relationship with Prospective Candidates
- Step 6 Evaluate the Formal Agreement
- Step 7 Evaluate the Post-Agreement Relationship

Step 1

CLARIFY THE OBJECTIVES OF THE ALLIANCE

Note: In order to audit an alliance or evaluate an alliance prospect, a steering committee should be organized, as described under the subhead "Who Should Conduct the Audit?" on the first page in the section *Steps in Conducting a Strategic Alliance Audit (Manufacturing)*, Part 1.

BACKGROUND INFORMATION

Alliances are not strategic unless they contribute to the achievement of a company's overall objectives. There are a number of possible strategic objectives that can be achieved by developing alliances, including the seven goals below.

- Strategic goal 1: Identify and access new technologies and competencies.
- Strategic goal 2: Exploit new market opportunities quickly and effectively.
- Strategic goal 3: Build market position rapidly.
- Strategic goal 4: Survive by specializing.
- Strategic goal 5: Re-establish critical mass.
- Strategic goal 6: Achieve cost leadership.
- Strategic goal 7: Withdraw from the market in an orderly fashion.

In the "Questions" section below you will find a set of questions for each of these important strategic goals.

QUESTIONS

Strategic Goal 1: Identify and Access New Technologies and Competencies

- To ensure long-term competitive advantage, has the company deployed a variety of mechanisms to locate and exploit external sources of R&D to augment in-house commitments?

- Do these mechanisms include:
  - ❑ collaboration with university departments
  - ❑ collaboration with other research institutions
  - ❑ pre-competitive collaborative R&D to spread research resources more wisely
  - ❑ corporate venturing, or making systematic investments in emerging companies to gain a window on the technologies and market applications of the future
  - ❑ joint ventures and other forms of strategic partnership which enable a company to acquire new competencies by "borrowing" them from a company with leadership position?

Strategic Goal 2: Exploit New Market Opportunities Quickly and Effectively

- Have company leaders decided whether new opportunities are attractive enough to get involved with commercially?

- Will the company enter new markets through:
  - ❑ in-house development
  - ❑ licensing or sourcing product from an existing supplier
  - ❑ acquiring an existing company
  - ❑ joint venture with another company?

Strategic Goal 3: Build Market Position Rapidly

- In order to build market position rapidly, should the company supply the product on an OEM basis for rebadging and resale by other companies?

- In order to build market position rapidly, should the company create value added reseller networks, where a range of different companies are involved in tailoring or augmenting the product for distribution to specialized users in various vertical markets?

- In order to build market position rapidly, should the company establish local joint ventures, with or without manufacturing capability, to access export markets?

- In order to build market position rapidly, should the company make strategic investments in local partners?

- Will the company consider entry and growth strategies together – especially where new categories of product are being developed for sale to a market with a well defined customer base, or with well established international distribution channels?

Strategic Goal 4: Survive By Specializing

- Should the company adopt strategies which avoid direct competition with the market leaders?
- Should the company specialize in a specific market sector or sub-product area?
- Should the company switch to on–off contracts, in which scale economies are far less important?
- Should the company buy in key components on an OEM basis?
- Should the company become a subcontractor to the industry leaders?
- Should the company become a distributor for the industry leaders?

Note: Strategic alliances are important in the areas mentioned in each of the last three questions and can extend the ability of a company to compete as its markets mature.

Strategic Goal 5: Re-Establish Critical Mass

- Does the company find it impossible to compete with the industry leaders and remain totally independent?
- Are the company's options either disposal or some type of merger operations with another company?

Note: Where a business unit is too small to be internationally competitive, undertaking a partial merger with a comparable division of another company can help strengthen market position and provide adequate R&D funding.

Strategic Goal 6: Achieve Cost Leadership

- Have activities been pinpointed where sharing or subcontracting can reduce unit costs either by setting up combined operations with competitors, or by disposing of assets which can be reinvested more effectively elsewhere in the business?
- In order to carry out this kind of strategic cost reduction program effectively, is there a detailed understanding of the relationship between volume and cost in different parts of each of the company's businesses?
- Would it be possible to reduce unit costs by sourcing products from low cost suppliers?

- Have the cost benefits of subcontracting and collaboration been weighed against the strategic risks of dependence on others, and the encouragement of competitors?

Strategic Goal 7: Withdraw from the Market in an Orderly Fashion

- If the company is fighting a losing battle in gaining competitive advantage, should it sell the business to another company?
- If the company is fighting a losing battle in gaining competitive advantage, should it gradually wind down operations?
- If the company is fighting a losing battle in gaining competitive advantage, should it consider a partial merger?

The importance of these seven goals in the audit process is to help the steering committee evaluate the objectives of an existing or prospective audit. This is the first step in assessing the effectiveness of a particular alliance. The next is evaluating the plan for the alliance. The questions that follow in Step 2, Part 1 will help you to do this.

Step 2

EVALUATE THE PLAN FOR THE ALLIANCE

BACKGROUND INFORMATION

Once the objectives of the alliance have been assessed, a more detailed plan should be evaluated in terms of its ability to support the objectives of the alliance.

The "Questions" section below will help you work through the number of steps that can be taken to improve chances for success by improving the planning process.

QUESTIONS

- Will members of the steering committee examine how the proposed or existing partnership is meant to help achieve the strategic goals set for their business?
- Before proceeding with or revising the alliance, will the partnership be compared with easier alternatives in terms of:
  - ❑ cost
  - ❑ benefits
  - ❑ risks
  - ❑ speed of execution?

Note: Some possible alternatives include:

❑ developing the resources in house that would be gained through the partnership

❑ buying a company that would supply the same advantages

❑ pursuing a different strategy.

- Will the committee review an outline of the activities to be undertaken within the partnership and the resources required?
- Will the committee study the broader relationships with the rest of the company's businesses and the long-term strategic impact?
- Will resources need to be diverted from other areas in order to make the alliance work?
- How do customers and other stakeholders respond to the alliance?

- Will this study include interviews with:
  - ❏ major customers
  - ❏ industry experts?
- Will this study solicit the input of key people within the company?
- Is there a plan of how the relationship will be structured and managed to obtain optimum benefit?
- Will the alliance be more successful if ownership of the resulting enterprise is divided equally?
- If ownership is not divided equally, will every effort be made to develop a fair division of responsibility and ownership based on the contribution made by each of the partners?

Note: A recent study found that alliances are most successful when ownership of the resulting enterprise is divided equally. This is because shared ownership implies shared responsibility.

- Will diagramming the contributions required of and rewards available to both partners in the alliance help to clarify in the minds of the steering committee (and the partners) the expectations for the agreement?

Note: A model for financial arrangements and the impact of changes is shown in Figure 2, Step 2, Part 1.

The type of planning as outlined in the questions above is critical to the success of any strategic alliance, regardless of its purpose. The questions in Step 3, Part 1 below will help you to outline some of the general considerations that should be taken into account when searching for an alliance partner.

Step 3

SPECIFY PARTNER CRITERIA

BACKGROUND INFORMATION

Alliance partners should be assessed according to the following dimensions.

1 Company size and strength.

2 Culture.

3 Complementarity of business.

4 Management compatibility.

In the "Questions" section below you will find a set of questions for each of these four dimensions.

QUESTIONS

1. Company Size and Strength

- Should the large company engage in strategic alliances in order to tap new technologies or processes that have been developed in the small, entrepreneurial firm?
- Will the large company be able to develop new processes and products as rapidly as the small company?
- Will the large company be farther removed from the immediate market than new start ups?
- Will the small company pursue alliances that will provide a source of income and possible access to large markets, as well as a source of knowledge that may help to improve performance?
- Will a marriage between an extremely strong partner and a comparatively weak partner present problems?
- Will an alliance fail in which one partner is consistently strong in the functions it brings to the venture while the other is not strong?
- If one partner is weak, will managing the alliance be too great a distraction from improvements needed in other parts of the business?

Note: The most effective partnerships seem to develop when the largest company is no more than three times the size of the smaller company.

2. Culture

- In order for partners to cooperate effectively, do the companies have compatible values and beliefs?

- Will serious conflicts arise if one organization is highly bureaucratic while the other shuns policies and procedures?

Note: Because the collaborative venture will be made up of people from both parent companies, they should approach work from similar perspectives if the alliance is to be successful.

- Is flexibility conducive to a good alliance?

- Will both partners be willing and able to make concessions and compromises as their ability to contribute to the alliance changes?

- Will a partner be willing to accept the modifications required if the other company's ability to contribute changes?

- Is the ability to transfer skills conducive to a good alliance?

- Will the companies involved in the partnership be able to transfer skills?

- Will one of the companies involved in the partnership be able to implement the skills derived from the knowledge base offered by the other?

Note: A company that can receive but not transfer skills may not be able to integrate new staff from the partner company into its organization. A new company that can transfer but not receive skills usually has a top-down management style and may not adapt well to changes required by the other partner.

3. Complementarity of Business

- Will the partnership be effective if one company contributes a unique technology and the other provides access to a market previously untapped by the technology-bearing company?

- Will the partnership be effective if both companies collaborate on the development of new technology that is related to the core business of both partners, but does not directly compete with either business?

4. Management Compatibility

- Will the managers from each parent company have responsibility for the alliance to develop strong personal relationships?

- Will the initiation of these relationship take place during the process of investigating prospective partners?

Note: Executives should not underestimate the importance of personal chemistry in choosing alliance partners. These personal relationships will be vital to the resolution of problems that develop in the alliance at later stages.

Having specified partner criteria, the next step is to screen and investigate partners. The questions below, which relate to Step 4, Part 1, will help you to do this.

Step 4

SCREEN AND INVESTIGATE PARTNERS

BACKGROUND INFORMATION

In cases where the choice of a partner is not obvious, the following systematic approaches will ensure that executives have explored a wide range of possibilities.

1 Consulting industry experts.

2 Reviewing trade publications.

3 Consulting trusted customers or suppliers.

This should then be followed by:

4 Evaluating the suitability of each candidate.

The "Questions" section below will help you to look at each of these areas in turn.

QUESTIONS

1. Consulting Industry Experts

- Might analysts who are familiar with the industry be able to suggest companies who match the criteria outlined for the partnership?
- Might analysts who are familiar with the industry be able to provide input on the compatibility of potential partners once the list of prospects has been narrowed?

2. Reviewing Trade Publications

- Should reviewing trade publications include an electronic data base search for companies within appropriate industries?
- Should this search be narrowed by using key terms drawn from the profile developed for the ideal partner?

3. Consulting Trusted Customers or Suppliers

- Will those who work closely with the company be able to suggest partners who would provide the qualities needed for an effective alliance?

Once a list of prospective partners has been made, these prospective partners should be assessed against the criteria developed for the partnership (see Step 3, Part 1). Before evaluating the suitability of each candidate, the following questions may help to gain valuable background information.

- Will company literature be solicited from each of the candidates as a preliminary tool for evaluating their compatibility?
- Will industry experts, both inside and outside the company, be approached for their input into the decision?
- Will the list of candidates be narrowed to between three and five?
- Will executive-level representatives of the candidate company be contacted to assess interest and ability to provide what is required by the alliance?

4. Evaluating the Suitability of Each Candidate

Note: For those companies that appear on the short list of alliance partner candidates, the initiating company should engage in a considerable amount of due diligence research.

- Will research into the companies who appear on the short list include interviewing those companies' major customers?
- How well do the companies meet customer needs?
- Do the companies respond quickly and effectively to the demands of the market?
- Will research include obtaining a credit report for each of the final candidates?
- Will research include an evaluation of the distribution of sales for each of the candidates?
- Is the company overly dependent on one customer?
- Are the company's sales concentrated in markets to which your company wants to gain access?
- Will research include establishing the potential partner's reputation in the industry?
- Is the potential partner known for following through on agreements, or will the partner pose risks that your company should avoid?

- Does the potential partner have a reputation in terms of developing new technology?

- Do executives at the prospective partner seem interested in and committed to making an alliance work?

- Do the prospective partner's goals for the alliance match up with the objectives of your company?

When candidates compare favorably with the criteria set out for the audit, then it is time for the steering committee to evaluate the process and details of developing the detailed alliance agreement. The questions below, which relate to Step 5, Part 1, will help you to do this.

Step 5

ASSESS THE ALLIANCE AGREEMENT

BACKGROUND INFORMATION

An effective process for assessing the alliance agreement includes the following.

1 A letter of intent.

2 A business plan for the new venture.

3 A final agreement.

The "Questions" section below will help you to look at each of these areas in turn.

QUESTIONS

1. Letter of Intent

- Will the letter of intent outline the general goals and objectives of each of the parent companies for the alliance?
- Will the letter describe the form of the alliance and the contribution of each parent in general terms?

Note: The letter of intent should be agreed upon by executives from both companies.

2. Business Plan for the New Venture

- Will the business plan be developed by working with teams from each of the parent companies?
- Will the working teams be composed of people who will manage the new venture once it begins operation?
- Will the plan include information that would be provided in the plan for any new venture, including:
  - ❑ market analysis
  - ❑ a marketing plan
  - ❑ financial projections
  - ❑ descriptions of the management teams?

- Will research sources include data gathered from:
  - ❑ both parent companies
  - ❑ customers
  - ❑ industry experts
  - ❑ secondary sources, such as trade publications or on-line data bases?

- Will the business plan contain a detailed description of what the contributions of each of the partners will be?

- As the business plan evolves, will it be reviewed by executives from each of the parent companies at each major iteration?

Note: It may be useful to have the plan presented to the respective executives by a third neutral party as insurance that feedback given on the plan is honest.

3. Final Agreement

- Will the agreement be based on the needs of the venture rather than on the political maneuvering of the respective partners?

- Will changes be negotiated on the basis of personal relationships between representatives from each company rather than on the technicalities of the alliance agreement?

Having answered all the questions in this section, it's time to look at the questions relating to the final step in Part 1 of this audit.

Step 6

EVALUATE THE ABILITY OF THE ALLIANCE TO MEET CHANGING CONDITIONS

BACKGROUND INFORMATION

The hallmark of a successful alliance is one that changes over time. Assessing a company's performance in terms of the following seven rules will enable the steering committee to evaluate the alliance's ability to respond as conditions evolve.

1 Balance trust with self-interest.

2 Anticipate strategic conflicts.

3 Establish clear strategic leadership.

4 Learn flexible management.

5 Accommodate cultural differences.

6 Orchestrate technology transfer.

7 Learn from the partner's strengths.

The "Questions" section below will help you to look at each of these rules in turn.

QUESTIONS

1. Balance Trust with Self-Interest

- Is there a mutual understanding of the partner's business?
- Does the company know what the other partner is capable of delivering?
- Is there a mutual appreciation of the partner's objectives?
- Are there good personal relationships?
- Are the partner's short-term objectives understood?

Note: The partner's objectives need to be understood because it is important that they be achieved.

- Do all partners feel that they stand to benefit?

- Will partners try to look at how the partnership fits into the other company's long-term strategy?

- Are the other company's aspirations with regard to the partner's business or markets known?

Note: Getting to know the partner's key personnel socially early on helps ensure that any potential difficulties can be aired frankly and solved in an atmosphere of mutual self-interest.

2. Anticipate Strategic Conflicts

- Will the company entering a strategic partnership try to identify the potential for conflicts and second-guess any hidden agendas that a partner might have?

- Will partners look carefully at the other parent's overall strategy and at any other partnerships in which the other business may be involved?

Note: Understanding where potential conflicts exist can help establish areas where action must be taken to reduce competitive risks.

- Where a formal joint venture is formed, will the scope of business be very clearly defined, to make sure that the potential competition with the parent companies can be managed effectively?

- Will the audit look at any apparent leaks in the system?

Note: Any strategic partnership is somewhat like a semi-permeable membrane through which technology and expertise can flow unintentionally from the stronger partner to the weaker.

- Will the audit consider the partner's access to resources and personnel?

- Will the limits of the relationship be defined to ensure that staff know what information can be shared and what information cannot?

3. Establish Clear Strategic Leadership

- In order to establish clear strategic leadership, will an independent entity headed up by a strong, politically adept chief executive or project director be created?

- In order to establish clear strategic leadership, will one of the partners take on the role of project management?

4. Learn Flexible Management

- Will the company ensure that all members of the team understand the importance of working with the other partner constructively?
- At the same time, will the limits of cooperation be clear?
- Will sensitive information be identified and isolated?

Note: Companies must be prepared to demand tighter control or change partners if the partnership is not delivering the benefits sought.

5. Accommodate Cultural Differences

- Will the audit process include evaluating a partner's business culture?
- Will the audit process include evaluating the ability of both companies to resolve cultural differences?
- Does the company know how the partner makes decisions and where the limits of authority lie?
- Does the company understand the partner's procedure for planning and measuring performance?
- Does the company understand the partner's rules for social and business behavior?

Note: Although companies should seek partners with appropriate cultural characteristics, bridging cultural gaps requires understanding and forbearance. It is important that all members of the partnership team know what is involved.

6. Orchestrate Technology Transfer

- Will a technology transfer plan be available to ensure that the technology developed is brought back into the sponsoring company, and that its commercial potential is well promoted internally?
- Will each partner have a strong "receptor" team with the technical skills to understand and use the technology?
- Will contact with the receptor team increase as the technical and marketing uncertainties are reduced and the technology or product comes closer to commercial exploitation?

7. Learn from the Partner's Strengths

- Will a strategic partnership offer the opportunity to observe how another company:
  - ❑ manages its R&D programs
  - ❑ organizes its business development program
  - ❑ operates its management information systems
  - ❑ manages its overseas subsidiaries
  - ❑ determines its remuneration packages?
- Will partners in an alliance be evaluated in terms of their ability and willingness to learn?
- Will at least some of the individuals involved in strategic partnerships be chosen for:
  - ❑ their receptivity to new ideas
  - ❑ their ability to disseminate what they have learned throughout the organization?
- Will internal seminars be set up to spread this knowledge?
- Will special programs be created to evaluate the relevance of this knowledge to the company's particular circumstances?
- Will career patterns be planned to ensure that ideas are rapidly passed on and implemented in key locations?

Note: Direct experience teaches most effectively. The more effective mechanisms there are for people to be involved in the learning experience that strategic partnerships provide, the sooner change will be made back home.

Now that you have answered the questions in Part 1, which relate to a manufacturing strategic alliance audit, you should look at how to conduct a strategic alliance audit for service firms. The questions that relate to the seven steps in Part 2 will help you to do this.

Step 1

DETERMINE THE APPROPRIATE TYPE OF ALLIANCE

Note: Advice on who should carry out the audit can be found under the subhead "Who Should Conduct the Audit?" on the first page in the section *Steps in Conducting a Strategic Alliance Audit (Services)*, Part 2.

BACKGROUND INFORMATION

An alliance will perform according to its purpose and structure. There are four types of alliances for services companies.

1 New-to-the-world alliances.

2 Service offering expansion alliances.

3 Customer base expansion alliances.

4 Sequential service offerings alliances.

The "Questions" section below covers each of these alliances in turn.

QUESTIONS

1. New-to-the-World Alliances

- Will development of new services through an alliance offer less control than internal development?

- Will development of new services through an alliance reduce each partner's need to invest in:
  - ❑ market research
  - ❑ concept development
  - ❑ service offering development
  - ❑ development of the capabilities to perform, market and sell a new service?

Note: Examples of this type of alliance are shown under the subhead "New-to-the-World Alliances" in Step 1, Part 2.

2. Service Offering Expansion Alliances

- Will this type of alliance permit the company to offer new services supplied by an alliance partner, either sold through their own sales efforts, or sold in tandem with their partner's sales effort?

Note: Examples of this type of alliance are shown under the subhead "Service Offering Expansion Alliances" in Step 1, Part 2.

3. Customer Base Expansion Alliances

- Will this form of alliance permit partners to:
  - ❑ surmount barriers to entry
  - ❑ coordinate distribution systems
  - ❑ develop a joint sales force?

Note: Examples of this type of alliance are shown under the subhead "Customer Base Expansion Alliances" in Step 1, Part 2.

4. Sequential Service Offerings Alliances

- Will these alliances permit companies to work together to coordinate a sequence of services?

- Will this type of alliance provide for coordination of services where there is a required sequence in which the services must be performed?

Note: Examples of this type of alliance coordination are shown under the subhead "Sequential Service Offerings Alliances" in Step 1, Part 2.

Each of these four major types of services alliance are noted in Figure 3, Step 1, Part 2. Other types of alliance are briefly covered at the end of Step 1, Part 2. Once you have determined the appropriate type of alliance for your company, the next step is to determine customer requirements and establish audit criteria. The questions below, which relate to Step 2, Part 2, will help you to do this.

Step 2

DETERMINE CUSTOMER REQUIREMENTS AND ESTABLISH AUDIT CRITERIA

BACKGROUND INFORMATION

Successful service alliances provide the end customer with better value (new services, lower cost, higher quality, reduced time, etc.). Therefore, an audit of alliance effectiveness must carefully identify, and if possible quantify, the factors that are of value to the end customer.

The "Questions" section below will help you to ascertain the establishment of criteria for evaluating the alliance.

QUESTIONS

- Will determining customer requirements involve:
  - ❏ surveys (in the case of broad markets with many customers)
  - ❏ discussions with specific customers (in the case of narrow markets with few customers)?
- Will these enquiries focus on broad customer needs, such as what services the customer would like to buy that are not currently offered by either the parent companies or the alliance?
- Will auditors also tap other important sources of information, such as prospective customer groups and industry experts?

Note: Good sources of general information about the market niche that the alliance competes in include:

❏ trade journals

❏ trade show participation

❏ commercial market data.

- In order to assess customer needs, will specific requirements that may bar customers from buying the output of an existing or proposed alliance be identified?

Note: Individual customers may place restrictions on the type of company that can be part of an alliance.

- Once research about general market demands has been completed, will the audit team outline the basic requirements of the alliance?

- Will these requirements be outlined both in terms of customer needs and in terms of the kind of alliance partner that would make the greatest contribution to the alliance?

Note: These criteria can most easily be established by first clarifying the objectives and purposes of the alliance.

- Will criteria be developed that consider:
  - ❏ what types of markets should be served
  - ❏ types of services to provide
  - ❏ whether the service should be fully developed from the outset or whether they should be developed as part of the alliance
  - ❏ the geographic area(s) of interest and exclusion
  - ❏ sales goals
  - ❏ financial criteria (returns) and the ability of the partners to invest
  - ❏ date of first commercial sale
  - ❏ leveragable strengths of the initiating firm
  - ❏ leveragable strengths needed in the alliance partner(s)
  - ❏ size of the alliance partner?

Once the criteria for partner selection have been established, they can be used to audit the quality of the existing relationship, or to search for a new partner for a prospective alliance. The process will be described through the questions below, which relate to Step 3, Part 2.

Step 3

EVALUATE SUITABILITY OF CURRENT OR POTENTIAL PARTNERS

BACKGROUND INFORMATION

In the case of existing alliances, partners with whom the initiating company is involved should be evaluated in terms of their appropriateness for the alliance being pursued.

In the case of new alliances, every effort should be made to select partners that most closely approach the ideal. The specific criteria outlined in Step 2, Part 2 should be taken into consideration, along with the ability to contribute equally to the alliance, plus common values and business priorities, as outlined at the beginning of Step 3, Part 2.

Successfully evaluating suitability of current or potential partners requires that the following sequence occurs.

1 Identifying prospective partners.

2 Screening candidates against the alliance criteria.

3 Research partner candidates.

4 Evaluation of the final candidates.

The "Questions" section below asks questions that relate to each part of this sequence in turn.

QUESTIONS

1. Identifying Prospective Partners

- In order to ensure that a partner or prospective partner is the ideal candidate for the alliance, will the audit team generate a long list of possible candidates?

- Will this list be created by using:
  - ❑ trade magazines (advertisements and editorial material)
  - ❑ buyers' guides
  - ❑ electronic (database) literature searching
  - ❑ trade associations
  - ❑ trade shows

- ❑ interviews with experts (both within and outside the initiating company)
- ❑ interviews with customers?

Key customers and customer groups may also be good sources to suggest appropriate alliance partners. Names generated in this way may include firms that already supply services to customers, or that have done so in the past.

2. Screening Candidates Against the Alliance Criteria

- Can the initial list generated by the audit team be trimmed without the expense of extensive research?
- Will candidates be screened against the criteria repeatedly as more information is gathered?
- Will the list of prospects be continually revised until a few candidates who meet the criteria remain?

3. Research Partner Candidates

- Will credit reports be run on selected firms?

Note: The diagram in Figure 5, Step 3, Part 2 illustrates possible information sources and shows how they interlock to complete the profile of each partner candidate.

4. Evaluation of the Final Candidates

- Once the two or three most suitable partners have been identified, will the results of the research be compiled and assessed against the original criteria set out for the alliance, as well as the prospective partner's ability to work well with the initiating company?

Some of the following questions (used to interview representatives from the prospective partner's customer base) should be taken into account when evaluating the final candidates.

- How well does the company meet its customer needs?
- Have customers asked for the addition of service features that have been ignored or denied?
- How healthy are the prospective partners?

- Are they overly dependent on one customer?
- How stable is their financial performance?
- Do the candidates have a good reputation in their industry?
- Are they known for following through on their agreements, or do they pose risks that alliance partners would want to avoid?
- Do they have a service reputation that the initiating company would want to be linked to?
- Is there the potential for a good personal relationship between executives from the prospective partner companies?
- Do their goals for the alliance match up with the objectives of the initiating company?
- What other alliances are the partners or prospective partners involved in?
- How would this affect the alliance being audited?

Once good candidates have been identified and investigated through a variety of sources, they should be approached about their interest in developing an alliance. Questions relating to this are given in the next step.

Step 4

INITIATE RELATIONSHIPS WITH SELECTED CANDIDATES

BACKGROUND INFORMATION

Careful steps should be taken to set up an appropriate introduction of the two companies in cases where the executives of prospective partners are unknown by executives from the initiating firm.

The brief list of questions that follows will help you to do this.

QUESTIONS

- Will an introduction of the two companies be best undertaken through a party known by managers, executives or owners of both firms?

Note: The ability to use others known to both companies underscores the importance of using those knowledgeable about the industry in addition to printed sources to generate lists of prospective partners.

- Where the potential alliance can provide significant benefit to specific customers, should common customers introduce alliance candidates?
- If this is not possible, should a formal letter be sent by your company to the candidate firm, giving:
  - ❑ background on the company
  - ❑ reasons for interest in a potential alliance?
- Will the letter be followed up by a phone call to arrange a personal meeting?

Because alliance relationships are often complex and intense, there are some aspects of a partnership that cannot be explored without actually developing a relationship between partner companies. The questions below, which relate to Step 5, Part 2, will help you to do this.

Step 5

DEVELOP A RELATIONSHIP WITH PROSPECTIVE CANDIDATES

BACKGROUND INFORMATION

Once executives from the prospective partner companies have been introduced, representatives from the companies should engage in a courtship process, as follows, to determine whether or not an alliance between the firms will be mutually beneficial.

1 Issues to address in the courtship process.

2 Establishing personal relationships.

The "Questions" section below will look at each of these in turn.

QUESTIONS

1. Issues to Address in the Courtship Process

- Is this partner trustworthy?
- What are the readily apparent benefits of the alliance to each partner?
- How will the corporate cultures (ethics, operating style, objectives) of the alliance partners mesh or clash?

Note: Executives considering an alliance should put themselves in the shoes of the prospective partner and evaluate the benefits of the alliance to both sides. Only mutually beneficial alliances tend to succeed.

- Will the relationship be accepted by key executives, managers, and other employees of both partners?
- Will the relationship be accepted by key players in the industry or market?
- Have the details of the venture been sufficiently explained throughout the organization?

Note: Early disclosure is sometimes limited in publicly held companies by stock market considerations.

- Has information about the alliance been presented in enough detail to ensure that everyone sees the work that will be required in the future?

- Has the team structure been established to work together on the alliance?

Note: This team should include representatives from each of the partner companies who will be involved in the management of the venture resulting from the alliance. This ensures that the alliance will be planned in a way that will contribute to the achievement of its objective.

- Has a joint business plan been prepared and realistically reviewed?

Note: The plan should be prepared by working teams from the partner companies. It should be reviewed by executives from the partner companies.

2. Establishing Personal Relationships

- Will the people chosen to establish the alliance be:
  - ❑ cooperative
  - ❑ open and trustworthy
  - ❑ competent and helpful
  - ❑ friendly and social
  - ❑ fair and easy to work with
  - ❑ rational decision makers
  - ❑ respected by others inside and outside the company?
- Will the people chosen to establish the alliance have a broad understanding of company operations?

Experience shows that the development of good personal relationships between representatives from the partner companies is much more important to the success of the venture than the terms of the formal agreement. However, a formal agreement still needs to be evaluated, and the questions that follow, which relate to Step 6, Part 2, will help you to do this.

Step 6

EVALUATE THE FORMAL AGREEMENT

BACKGROUND INFORMATION

You will need to ask a number of key questions at this stage of alliance development. These questions are listed below.

QUESTIONS

- Can the contribution of each party be structured so as to avoid conflicts?
- Are there adequate exit provisions?
- If the alliance fails, what does each party retain?
- Do both sides understand what each party is trying to achieve from the alliance?
- Who will be the key competitors?
- Who is to do what, and by when, and what will happen if it is not done?
- Have the agreements been carefully defined, with consideration for guaranteed minimum, maximum royalties, audits, penalties if payments are delayed and taxation issues?

Note: If licensing or royalty agreements are involved, estimating the value of these agreements is difficult.

* Have intellectual property rights been clearly addressed?

Critical elements of the arrangement should be concluded before the formal agreement is written. Then it is time to study the final step in Part 2, which is how to evaluate the post-agreement relationship.

Step 7

EVALUATE THE POST-AGREEMENT RELATIONSHIP

BACKGROUND INFORMATION

An assessment of the following aspects of alliance management can help audit team members evaluate possible improvement strategies for an existing audit. It can also suggest safeguards that should be taken in the design of a new alliance.

1 Key questions in managing alliances.

2 Balance between the partners.

3 Ability to learn from alliance partners.

4 Cultural compatibility.

The questions below will help you to evaluate each of these aspects.

QUESTIONS

1. Key Questions in Managing Alliances

- Does the alliance have a clear identity?
- Do employees, customers and suppliers know who or what the alliance really is?
- Has this identity changed over time to address the changing needs of customers and other stakeholders?
- Is there too much focus on internal alliance issues and not enough focus on the customer and competition?
- Have the key marketing and sales issues been adequately addressed?
- How will the new service be sold?

Note: Information relating to each of the questions above can be found under the subhead "Key Questions in Managing Alliances" in Step 7, Part 2.

The next three aspects all relate to the long-term issues in alliance management. The questions will help you to evaluate the performance (or potential) of an alliance for each issue.

2. Balance between the Partners

- Is ownership of the alliance equally shared?

- Do the partners make equal contributions or trades in terms of:
  - ❑ money
  - ❑ resources
  - ❑ people
  - ❑ technology
  - ❑ skill
  - ❑ access to markets?

- Is the alliance evaluated on a regular basis to ensure that changes in the strengths and interests of each of the partners are reflected in the ownership arrangement?

Note: The information under the subhead "Balance between the Partners" in Step 7, Part 2, will help you to answer these questions in relation to your own situation.

3. Ability to Learn from Alliance Partners

- Is the initiating company willing to integrate ideas learned from the other partner in the management alliance?

- Is the initiating company willing to offer management ideas that will improve the performance of the alliance?

- Are the partners willing to integrate ideas from other companies in the management alliance?

- Are the partners willing to offer management ideas that will improve the performance of the alliance?

Note: The information under the subhead "Ability to Learn from Alliance Partners" in Step 7, Part 2, will help you to answer these questions in relation to your own situation.

4. Cultural Compatibility

- What are the similarities and differences between the culture of the initiating company and those of its current or prospective alliance partners?

- How will these differences affect the business of the particular alliance?
- Have mechanisms been discussed for resolving cultural differences that arise in the management of the alliance?

Note: The information under the subhead "Cultural Compatibility" in Step 7, Part 2, will help you to answer these questions in relation to your own situation.

IN CONCLUSION ...

The questions in this section of the audit guide will help you to establish where alliance performance can be improved. The extensive explanations in Parts 1 and 2 will help you to answer these questions to best effect.

Good luck!

***Parts 1 and 2*: David Connell** *is a consultant at The Technology Partnership in London.* **Ken Wexler** *has assisted North American and European companies with their alliance and acquisition strategy and implementation. He is president of New Business Search & Development International Corporation, with offices in Old Saybrook, Connecticut and Breda, Holland.* **Peter J. LaPlaca** *is Professor of Marketing at the University of Connecticut. His research interests include analysis of strategic alliances for manufacturing companies and business-to-business service providers.* ***Part 3** has been adapted from* The Company AuditGuide *published by Cambridge Strategy Publications Ltd.* ***Part 4** has been developed by Cambridge Strategy Publications Ltd.*